D0014449

THE
EVOLUTION
OF
REVOLUTIONS

THE
EVOLUTION
OF
REVOLUTIONS

HOW WE
CREATE, SHAPE, AND
REACT TO CHANGE

PATRICK J. HOWIE

59 John Glenn Drive
Amherst, New York 14228-2119

Published 2011 by Prometheus Books

Inquiries should be addressed to
Prometheus Books
59 John Glenn Drive
Amherst, New York 14228–2119
VOICE: 716–691–0133
FAX: 716–691–0137
WWW.PROMETHEUSBOOKS.COM

15 14 13 12 11   5 4 3 2 1

Library of Congress Cataloging-in-Publication Data

Howie, Patrick J., 1970–.
    The evolution of revolutions : how we create, shape, and react to change / by Patrick J. Howie.
        p. cm.
    Includes bibliographical references and index.
    ISBN 978–1–61614–235–3 (cloth : alk. paper)
    1. Revolutions. 2. Technological innovations. 3. Creative ability. I. Title.

HM876.H69 2011
303.48'4—dc22

2010043641

Printed in the United States of America on acid-free paper

*To my wife, Samantha,
and my children, Ryan and Lauren*

CONTENTS

FOREWORD

As a professor of marketing for more than three decades at the Harvard Business School and the Wharton School of the University of Pennsylvania, I used stories—we called them *case studies*—and the Socratic method to create valuable, sustainable knowledge for our students. I used case studies not as a supply-side teaching strategy that favors the instructor, but as a demand-side learning device that favors the student. As in schools of medicine and law, my business school case studies engaged the emotions of MBAs and executives. Business schools are not regarded as being in the entertainment business, but emotions can be a means to an end. To succeed, knowledge must increase, and effective behaviors must be adopted. In the classroom, the case method challenged present and future captains of industry, as well as me, to convert emotion and isolated experiences into sustainable excellence.

Author Patrick J. Howie is a superb practitioner of the case method. There are important lessons to be learned here, and Howie is a superb teacher. He shows how revolutions occur and how evolutionary processes enabled them. His work applies to all who seek success in their chosen fields.

First of all, he has the tools. He's a big-picture visionary and master storyteller. He's engaging. He's authoritative. He builds on evidence. He documents his sources. He's not making this up. He tells what happened, how it happened, and what it means to us. He has the rare ability to deconstruct complexity and make it accessible and exciting to the lay reader. He can do this without resorting to a single chart, table, or graph. Where others see points, he sees patterns. Where others see pictures, he sees videos. Where others see serial events, he sees parallels, convergences, and connections.

Second, he has chosen a fascinating subject. His work reveals original insights into the conditions and causes of ideas of such power that they literally revolutionized thinking in their respective areas of inquiry.

To borrow from today's newsgathering and dissemination trade: in any important pursuit, there are headlines and there are stories. Revolutions in science, technology, and intranational politics are headline events. They become unforgettable moments in history.

By contrast, Howie argues the stories that precede, accompany, and follow historic headlines are vital to the revolutionary explosion. These stories are literally the fore and aft of revolution. With the passage of time, stories become overshadowed by enduring memories of the revolution itself and eroded from popular memory by the news of the day. Generations later, most of us have lost awareness of the progressive contexts of seemingly sudden successes.

This is most unfortunate. Evolutionary stories have much to teach us about the persons and personalities who ultimately were responsible for successful revolutions. Stories of evolution disclose ambitions, frustrations, processes, and concepts that were relevant then and are relevant today.

Howie's thoroughly researched and engagingly recounted stories of forgotten evolutions surprise and reward us. He engages our emotions, fuels our passions, increases our knowledge, and challenges us to take action. His well-told narratives help us as individuals and groups. Separately and together we will feel, learn, and subsequently behave with greater insight and improved chances of success.

Regardless of your field of endeavor, he will help you focus your vision, talent, and collaborative abilities to develop your opportunities to their highest potential. In the end, ongoing stories drive the occasional headline. Patrick has a great story to tell. With his insights, you'll write your own headline.

Stewart DeBruicker, PhD

Philadelphia
May 2010

INTRODUCTION

A Revolutionary Book

"This makes a lot of sense . . . at least on paper"[1]
—a blogger's assessment of electronic books

Paper or Electronic? Did you know that by the very act of reading this book you are helping to shape a revolution? The electronic book or, more precisely, the electronic book *reader* nudged its way into the public consciousness in the 2009 holiday season. To the general public, the e-reader was no longer that obscure toy they heard about at cocktail parties. The Amazon Kindle was entering its third holiday season, and the buzz surrounding the early 2010 release of the Apple iPad reached near-deafening levels. While the e-reader was still a product for those ahead of the curve, much like flat-screen televisions were a few years before, more and more people started to *consider* owning one.

The holiday season proved to be successful, at least according to Amazon CEO Jeff Bezos, who triumphantly claimed that the Amazon Kindle was "the most gifted" item in Amazon's history and that sales of e-books outstripped sales of regular books on Christmas day.[2] Just over a month later, the iPad was officially introduced to the world, although it took another three months before it was actually available for purchase. Apple reported over 300,000 sales of the iPad on the first day alone and over 250,000 books purchased from the Apple iBook store within the first few days.[3]

Despite this heightened fanfare, the e-book and the e-reader have a long and storied history. The first e-books were produced by the nonprofit organization Project Gutenberg all the way back in 1971 with the simple mission "to encourage the creation and distribution of eBooks."[4] The e-book received a boost in 2000 when Stephen King made his new book, *Riding the Bullet*, available in electronic form only.[5] Shortly before King's release, thirty-two organizations representing the publishing and technology industries teamed up to develop e-book standards.[6]

The e-book community noted that the computer was not perfectly suited for book reading since the computer, even the laptop, was not light and portable enough for most reading, not to mention that the text was difficult to read. Recognizing a need, numerous companies developed e-readers in the early part of the decade. Midway through the decade, the big boys joined the party as Sony launched its first e-reader to much fanfare in 2006 and Amazon launched the first Kindle in November of 2007. Apparently unprepared for the pent-up demand, the Kindle sold out in one day and was out of stock for the next five months.[7] Despite this setback, first-year sales of Kindles were actually larger than first-year sales of Apple's iPod.[8]

Although "traditional" books still dominate the market, all the signs indicate that the publishing industry is in the early stages of a revolution. This revolution will extend well beyond the mere replacing of paper with electrons as the technology will continue to develop into areas that we can only imagine today. This revolution will also fundamentally alter the publishing industry, as the balance of power across publishers and with authors will change radically. How and when this revolution takes place depends, in part, on how you—the reader and consumer—respond to these developments.

This book will explore how innovations develop and what must transpire for an innovation to create a revolution. Along the way we will explode some of the myths about innovation and revolutions, namely, that innovations occur as a result of the superhuman abilities of individuals or that revolutions occur in a single great leap. In their place, this book will demonstrate how innovations and revolutions are social phenomena that require overcoming many powerful psychological and communal forces.

Creative destruction is the process by which new ideas, businesses, and industries emerge and therefore lead to the downfall of traditional ideas, businesses, and industries. It is a revolutionary process. A revolution is not just a political event, for revolutions occur in all areas, whether in business, politics, or science, but the revolutionary process for all areas is the same. Revolutions represent a long process—from the initial innovation to the dramatic revolutionary period, through the long postrevolutionary adjustment. At its core, this book is about understanding the process of innovation and how a new idea, product, or service spreads throughout a social system to cause a revolution. The goal here is to enable the reader to identify or create revolutions as well as to capitalize on the effects of revolutions.

This is a business book, but it is not about business. It takes a wide-angle view of innovation as a social phenomenon rather than a narrow view of its being exclusively a business innovation. But this book does adopt an important element from the traditional business model of learning, the case study. I have evaluated over two dozen revolutions, most of which will be discussed throughout the book. But three will be discussed in detail, both to highlight the universal nature of the process of innovation and change, regardless of the subject matter, as well as to bring together a unified way of looking at the revolutionary process across the political, scientific, and economic spheres. What you will find is that the process of innovation and change is surprisingly similar across all these seemingly distinct fields.

Rather than pull some specific case studies only from industry, however, we will focus on three of the largest forces that have shaped, and that continue to shape, our world and culture: the democratic revolution that began with the American Revolution, the relativity revolution that took hold through Albert Einstein's theories, and the seemingly rapid emergence of the World Wide Web as the dominant social force of our time. These case studies have been chosen not only because they represent fascinating stories and highlight facts that may surprise many. They have been chosen because among their many similarities is the fact that the common view of each story is wrong.

For example, the idea that each of these revolutions was the work of a single act of genius or reflected a dramatic leap forward in thinking is an unfortunate oversimplification. Each of these revolutions evolved over decades and represented the culmination of a social process. In addition, the "revolutionary" moment so often mythicized will be shown to be only an intermediate step in the process, as the revolution continued well beyond that moment.

Although *The Evolution of Revolutions* focuses on these major events, it will be clear by the end of the book that innovation, change, and "revolutions" are occurring all the time and can revolve around the smallest of items. In any industry today, there are multiple revolutions occurring. Granted, some are more significant than others, but innovation and change is occurring constantly. The same is true inside a company—

inside every company today there are multiple revolutions occurring. These revolutions could reflect a change in how a product is manufactured, how a sales force is structured, or how a business process is changed to address a specific problem. While these are generally not thought of as "revolutions," the process of innovation and change is the same from the smallest "revolution" to the largest political, scientific, or economic revolution.

Our aim is to show how the story of these revolutions can help people understand how to identify, create, and react to revolutions. Separating the case study chapters are chapters that focus on helping readers harness the power of innovations. Innovation isn't easy. By understanding the process of innovation and how innovations throughout history have sparked lasting revolutions, readers will learn how to create revolutions of their own.

At the heart of any revolution are one or more innovations. Critical to creating, leading, or exploiting revolutions is the ability to understand how innovations are developed. I know all too well that creating novel solutions is a difficult task wrought with many failures, but I also know that some people and some organizations are much better at innovating than others. Being able to identify the critical elements of successful innovator teams and successful innovators is crucial to success. Drawing on my personal experience as well as research on creativity and innovation, this book will lay out the critical elements to creating successful innovations.

Creating *successful* innovations is actually very different from creating innovations, as the former requires acceptance by a target audience. A critical thesis of this book is that in order for an innovation to successfully cause a revolution, it must pass through three stages: resistance, clarification, and elaboration. Failure to pass through each stage is what separates a fad from a true revolution.

Recent advances in the psychology of decision making help us understand the motivating forces behind resistance. They also provide insight into what is required to overcome it. Two striking features emerge when we focus on resistance: first, resistance is a completely rational response to an innovation, even in the face of seemingly overwhelming evidence; second, the decision to adopt or reject an innovation is frequently not based on the evidence anyway. It is fascinating to learn that Einstein's theory of relativity actually had relatively little evidence as compared to Newtonian physics. Consequently, while a large portion of the physics community initially did not accept the newer theory, some members immediately gravitated to relativity despite the lack of evidence.

That new innovations are met with resistance is hardly a novel idea, but the notion that resistance leads to further refinements of the innovation is an often-misunderstood element in the transition from innovation to revolution. Despite the efforts of the smartest people, new innovations almost always have "bugs" that need to be worked out. This is one reason why it is natural to resist, since it is highly likely there is some problem that has yet to be detected. The ability to successfully improve the innovation or, in the rare case when the innovation is correct out of the gate, the ability to provide sufficient evidence that the innovation is fundamentally sound is critical to transforming an innovation into a revolution—this is the clarification stage.

A corollary to the ability to clarify exactly what the innovation does and the benefit it provides is the capability to extend the innovation to meet additional demands not originally foreseen. True innovations spark further innovations, and the resultant revolutions actually represent the cumulative impact of the initial innovations as well as the subsequent innovations. One of the fascinating facts that will clearly be demonstrated is that the value of the subsequent innovations always dwarfs the value of the original innovation. The real value of the original innovation lies in the ability to open new avenues for further innovation.

It has been noted that there is no shortage of good innovative ideas and that the ability to determine which innovative idea will lead to a revolution is a formidable challenge facing those in business, politics, or science. The final theme of this book focuses on the means of identifying those innovations that will lead to revolutions. I have spent the last fifteen years, first as an economist then as marketing scientist, with the primary objective in developing tools to forecast how new products, changes in regulations, or market conditions will impact consumer's choices. Based on this work as well as recent advances in marketing science, this book will link one of the most used forecasting tools to newly developed market research tools so as to provide clear guidance on how to detect future revolutions.

The ideas behind *The Evolution of Revolutions* follow a path strikingly similar to the book's core thesis: that a revolution is the result of a long developmental evolution, a "revolutionary moment," then a long period of further evolution that culminates in a synthesis of the innovation process.

The first seeds for this book were sown back while I was a

student at the University of Pennsylvania. I had taken a particular interest in political philosophy and, upon studying the great philosophical treatises that emerged during the Enlightenment period, I was rather shocked to see that the most beautiful language from the Declaration of Independence was plagiarized from these philosophical treatises. While this is well known to political scientists and philosophers, I have since learned that many people are not familiar with the intellectual heritage of the democratic revolution.

During those years I was also introduced to the fundamental shift in worldview that resulted from Einstein's physics, based on relativity, compared to that based on traditional Newtonian physics. I was stunned then, when I was reading a book by the French mathematician Henri Poincaré in which he actually introduced the term "relativity" a few years prior to Einstein and addressed the near crisis the physics community was facing when dealing with the struggle to integrate new information into the traditional Newtonian physics. Again, very few people outside of those who study the history of physics or the philosophy of science recognize that Einstein's breakthrough was not as radical as most are led to believe.

These two events represent striking examples of revolutionary ideas clearly being the result of evolutionary processes. Further evaluation of numerous other revolutions, both big and small, have reinforced that evolutionary processes are a fundamental component of revolutions. The study of other evolutions has also led me to see clear patterns and similarities across revolutions, regardless of the subject area. For example, research into the development of the World Wide Web identified a process similar to that of the democratic revolution and the relativity revolution. Most striking, the fundamental notion underlying the web—that of interconnectedness and the ability to sift through massive volumes of information to find that which is most relevant—was identified as a critical need back before the first computer was even completed. Again, the World Wide Web, which seemingly exploded onto the public consciousness in the late 1990s, was merely part of an evolutionary process for those within the information technology area.

The revolutionary moment that inspired *The Evolution of Revolutions* came out of a presentation I gave to a struggling "not-com" company in the early 2000s. The employees of this company truly believed they were going to revolutionize their industry, but they struggled with both internal and external resistance. Tensions ran high within the organization and among the senior management team, with finger pointing being the most common reaction to problems. Drawing on my research into the struggles faced by other organizations, I decided to put those struggles in context. My presentation was designed to encourage everyone to step back and recognize that the tensions and struggles we were experiencing were not unique to the company or the result of bad management but rather reflected the struggles that accompany innovation and change.

By showing that that company's struggles, both internal and external with clients, were no different than the struggles faced by others undergoing revolutions, the presentation enabled the extended management team, which included members from every group in the organization, to stop (or at least reduce) blaming others for their struggles and to recognize that creating change is exceptionally challenging. For me, however, that presentation inspired this book: going from a descriptive account of the struggles associated with creating change to an insightful and useful understanding of how to harness the forces of change.

Chapter 1

THE WORLD WIDE WEB PHENOMENON

As the year 2000 approached, the typical superlative lists were splashed everywhere, as were the ubiquitous "best of" reports. The cable television channel A&E got into the act with its own take on this subject, the "Biography of the Millennium." The channel polled over three hundred "scholars, world leaders, and journalists"[1] to determine who was the most influential person of the millennium. While these lists are always very entertaining, they are also very debatable and rife with potential biases.

This illustrious group had numerous potential high-profile and highly influential individuals throughout these one thousand years to choose from, including the major figures in science, such as Newton, Darwin, and Einstein; in politics and social thought, such as George Washington, Gandhi, and Karl Marx; and in the military, such as Napoleon Bonaparte, Adolph Hitler, and William the Conqueror. But the group selected none of these high-profile people as their most influential person of the millennium. Instead they chose the inventor Johannes Gutenberg.

Johannes Gutenberg was born in Germany in 1398, reinvented movable type and the printing press in the middle of the fifteenth century (movable type had already been invented in China four hundred years ago), and printed the first version of the famous Gutenberg bible in 1453.[2] While Gutenberg went bankrupt a few years later, the significance of his invention was quickly recognized, and he was given the title "gentleman of the court" in 1465.[3]

While it is unclear exactly whether Gutenberg ever profited from his invention, the printing press was a huge success. By 1470 the first printing press was set up at the Sorbonne in Paris, and by 1501 there were over one thousand printing presses that had produced over thirty-five thousand books and over ten million total copies.[4] What makes the printing press so valuable? Quite simply, it is the fact that it dramatically increases the dissemination of knowledge. An intellectual advance developed in one small area of the globe now had a much greater chance of reaching others with similar interests and ideas, even in far-flung parts of the globe. The printing press was the fourteenth-century equivalent of the World Wide Web.

In addition to the publication and widespread dissemination of the classic works of Aristotle, Plato, and other Greek scholars, a new crop of influential thinkers were able to inspire others to generate new ideas. It wasn't long before Thomas More published his groundbreaking book *Utopia*, which laid out a vision of an ideal society that differed in innumerable ways from European society of the time, and Niccolò Machiavelli published *The Prince*, which presented a stark account of the means to gaining power.[5] The printing press is arguably the driving force behind the spread of Renaissance thought, which began in Italy in the fourteenth century and culminated in the Enlightenment.

In another similarity to the World Wide Web, the printing press dramatically increased the number of people who had the ability to publish their own insights as well as to read the published works of others. Prior to the printing press, very few individuals owned any books, and the books that were owned were primarily in religious libraries. Slowly, the wealthy began to purchase books for their own personal libraries. Eventually, some personal libraries became larger than most religious libraries. Soon, the largest libraries were to be found at the relatively novel institution—the university. The first modern universities began shortly after the turn of the last millennium. By the time of the invention of the printing press, there were a couple of dozen universities in Europe. The printing press enabled these universities to greatly expand the intellectual opportunities available to their students.

The rate of acceleration of new ideas and discoveries that began with the Renaissance, which we naturally ascribe to individuals, derived in fact from the broad community in which these individuals were "interacting." The book, pamphlet, and (to a lesser extent) newspaper became the de facto social channels that dramatically increased the transfer of knowledge even among individuals who did not know each other. Today, the World Wide Web is leading to an even greater acceleration of this social process. Moreover, the story of how the web came to be provides a compelling case study into how real revolutions occur.

Although the web itself is barely a decade old, the inspiration behind its development goes all the way back to 1945. The year 1945 is significant for many reasons, not the least of which is because it marked the end of World War II. It is also the year the first computer was built. ENIAC, which is the abbreviation for the Electronic Numeric Integrator and Calculator,[6] was built at the University of Pennsylvania and completed in the fall of 1945.

The US Army commissioned ENIAC three years earlier as a

faster and more reliable approach to calculating what are known as firing tables. Since the path of a bullet or any piece of artillery is affected by numerous factors, including wind, temperature, distance to target, and the type of gun, World War II gunners were provided with a firing table to determine the correct firing angle. For every trajectory, a mathematical equation needed to be solved that would determine the appropriate angle based on the combined effect of all of these factors.[7] Traditionally these calculations were completed by "computers," a term that originally referred to people who solved equations.[8]

The demand for firing tables quickly became an issue of critical importance to the United States' war effort. A typical firing table included three thousand trajectories, and each trajectory took about one to two days to calculate by a human "computer."[9] Since a separate firing table needed to be calculated for each type of geography (e.g., a firing table built for France did not work in Africa) and for each type of gun, the human calculators could not keep up with the demand. To solve this problem, John Mauchly, an assistant professor at the University of Pennsylvania, proposed to build an electronic calculating machine for the army. The army accepted the proposal in 1942, but the project proved more difficult than had been expected, and it took over three years to complete. Ironically, despite being commissioned by the army for the war, ENIAC was not completed until after the war ended.

Perhaps even more ironic, the vision of the future of the digital age that would lead to the development of the World Wide Web was laid out prior to the completion of ENIAC. This vision was the product of Vannevar Bush, chief scientific advisor to President Roosevelt and director of the Office of Scientific Research and Development during World War II. This vision was presented in his seminal *Atlantic Monthly* (with an abbreviated version appearing in *LIFE* magazine) article, "As We May Think,"[10] which conveyed Bush's view of the future of computing power and information retrieval. This article articulated a vision that inspired the development of computers and computer networks for the next fifty years.

Vannevar Bush's importance to the development of the computer and the World Wide Web is barely recognized. Bush stood at the crossroads between the long line of development of the analog calculating machines—first envisioned by Charles Babbage in the early nineteenth century—and the dawning of the new digital age. Bush played a critical role in the development of analog calculating machines that led to the modern digital computer, and he had the foresight to see where these developments would take society today.

The original idea for an electronic computer—that is, a machine that could perform the calculations that have been historically done by teams of humans creating mathematical tables for numerous applications (including navigation and astronomy)—originated in the early 1800s with Charles Babbage.[11] Babbage was one of leading intellectuals of the early nineteenth century. He was the Lucasian Professor of Mathematics at Cambridge, which is the same position Isaac Newton held in the late seventeenth century and Steven Hawking holds today. Babbage famously convinced the British government to fund the development of his Difference Engine. The Difference Engine was to use the "method of differences," which requires only addition and subtraction to perform all calculations instead of the much more demanding multiplication and division. The Difference Engine was to leverage the mechanical advances rapidly occurring during the Industrial Revolution to create a machine that could replace the dozens of people typically required to calculate the necessary mathematical and logarithmic tables. The vision, however, preceded the technology, and after numerous years and the equivalent of millions of dollars spent, only a small prototype model was ever built.[12]

While in the process of building the Difference Engine, however, Babbage had an idea for a machine that could perform any type of calculation, not just those using the method of differences. He called this the Analytical Engine. Given the considerable investment by the British government in the unsuccessful Difference Engine, Babbage was not able to get any support for this second machine. Although he never gave up on his dream of making the Analytical Engine and he continued to develop the drafts for his machine throughout his life, he never attempted to actually build the Analytical Engine.[13]

Despite Babbage's failure to develop his Analytical Engine, the desire to automate the burdensome calculations required of an increasingly complex world persisted. As the wheels of progress rolled on during the height of the Industrial Revolution, manufacturing capabilities made great strides, and with these capabilities came the development of machines to perform all sorts of manual tasks to exacting standards. From the early 1800s through the early 1900s, machines such as the calculator, cash register, and typewriter were mass produced. Incidentally, if you ever wondered why the letters on a typewriter or computer are aligned in their current seemingly random fashion, then you need to go back to the development of the original typewriter. The first typewriter put the letters in alphabetical order, just as one would expect. However, the letterplates that were used to make their mark at the end of the mechanical arm tended to get jammed when two adjacent letters were pressed at about the same time. This occurred frequently with fast typists. To solve this jamming problem, the most popular letters were separated. The result is the famous

QWERTY in the upper left of the machine (It should be noted that vestiges of the original layout remain in the FGHJKL row—only the *I* was moved).[14]

Perhaps the most significant calculating machine to be invented in the early 1900s is the differential analyzer. The differential analyzer is an analog machine that could solve a whole class of difficult problems—ordinary differential equations. The inventor of this machine was none other than Vannevar Bush. Bush, who became an electrical engineering professor at MIT in 1919, built the differential analyzer in the late 1920s. While the differential analyzer was not mass produced, a few copies were made for other organizations, most notably the University of Pennsylvania and the US Army's Aberdeen Proving Ground in Maryland. During World War II the differential analyzer was used, along with scores of human "computers," to calculate the firing tables for the army. More important, the differential analyzer became an integral link between the University of Pennsylvania and the army,[15] which ultimately led to the development of ENIAC.

Bush's greatest influence on the development of both the computer and, ultimately, the World Wide Web was not through his creation of the differential analyzer, which represented one among a series of analog computing machines built over the prior century. Rather, it was his ability to have a vision for computing technology that inspired a generation of computer scientists. In his role as director of the Office of Scientific Research and Development, Bush oversaw nearly all the scientific developments that were funded by the government during the war, including the development of ENIAC and the Manhattan Project. As a result of his understanding of the numerous technological advances made during the war, Bush had a vision of what the future should be.

As the war was coming to an end, Bush recognized that the thousands of scientists who left their regular jobs to work on military projects would be reentering the workforce. Bush pointed these scientists toward the development of a technological solution to the problem of information overload. With the rapid pace of scientific and technological advancement, Bush wrote, the "investigator is staggered by the findings and conclusions of thousands of other workers—conclusions which he cannot find time to grasp, much less remember, as they appear. . . . Our methods of transmitting and reviewing the results of research are generations old and by now are totally inadequate for their purpose."[16] By way of example, Bush told the story of how Mendel's discovery of genetics was lost for a generation because it failed to be read by the few people who understood the implications. Bush feared that this problem was only getting worse. With a rapid acceleration in the total volume of output by scientists, he felt it was almost certain that numerous significant findings were being lost in the sea of potentially important but less-revolutionary research.

Despite the vast and rapidly increasing volume of new research, technological advances in information storage pointed toward an ability to store all of this research electronically (admittedly, Bush didn't conceive of the degree to which the technology of information storage would progress). But the use of modern technologies for storage was not Bush's issue. Bush was concerned with the ability to access the information, for, "a record, if it is to be useful to science, must be continuously extended, it must be stored, and above all *it must be consulted*" (emphasis added).[17]

Storing all the information in such a way as to be accessible (from a single location) is a necessary but not sufficient condition for improving scientists' ability to actually learn from—and expand on—the advances of other scientists. Scientists needed an efficient way to find the other research of interest. Astonishingly, Bush recognized that the solution to this problem was through the future of the still-incomplete computer.

The notion that the computer should be used to help man improve his ability to store and, more important, retrieve knowledge is a seemingly radical reconceptualization of the whole purpose of a computer. The goal of those trying to develop a computer, from the time of Babbage to that of ENIAC, was to develop a machine to automate mathematical calculations. At first blush, the only thing that separated the first computers from traditional calculators and other calculating devices was that they were electronic instead of mechanical. The benefit of using electronics is due to the increased speed available to performing calculations.[18]

But Bush was aware of the conceptual, mathematical, and technological developments that pointed to a bigger future for the computers. Bush understood that the computer really represented a fundamentally different approach to making calculations and that this new approach had wide-ranging applications. The real difference from the computer to old calculating machines was not that it was able to solve mathematical problems much more quickly (for each successive generation of calculating machine, including Bush's own differential analyzer, represented an increase in speed over previous generations) but rather because the computer could be used to solve problems of any kind.

The concept of a "universal" problem-solving machine was independently developed in the 1930s by Alonzo Church, a mathematics professor at Princeton University, and Alan Turing, a British mathematician who ultimately became leader of the English code-breaking team in World War II.[19] Although ENIAC was really a machine designed for a specific type of calculation, the team building it proposed building a successor (while still building ENIAC) called EDVAC, which made tangible the concept of a universal problem-solving machine. The proposal was written by John von Neumann, cofounder of game theory and one of the most esteemed mathematicians of his day. It was given to the military in June 1945, just one month before Bush's visionary article. This report, the *First Draft of a Report on the EDVAC*, has been hailed as the "most important document ever written on computing and computers."[20]

While the Von Neumann report laid out how to build a computer, which has guided the design of computers to this day, the Bush article, published only a month later, provided a vision for why to build a computer. Bush recognized that the computer could serve as a general-purpose information machine, not just a general-purpose calculating machine, and he championed the development of nonmathematical functions of computer technology. The subsequent rise of the computer industry can be viewed as following two paths: the first path follows Von Neumann and focuses on the use the computer to perform logical/mathematical calculations—which is how IBM came to dominate the business landscape; the second path follows Bush and focuses on using the computer to enhance the needs of humans—which developed in relative obscurity for decades until first the personal computer and later the Internet hit the public consciousness.

Bush's vision inspired the computer science industry for the next fifty years. He argued that the current system of finding information was inefficient and, more important, fundamentally did not match how humans search: "Our ineptitude in getting at the record is largely caused by the artificiality of systems of indexing. When data of any sort are placed in storage, they are filed alphabetically or numerically, and information is found (when it is) by tracing it down from subclass to subclass. . . . The human mind does not work that way. It operates by association. With one item in its grasp, it snaps instantly to the next that is suggested by the association of thoughts."[21] Bush famously postulated his "memex" as a device that could not only store vast amounts of information but would have a system of indexing that would allow the user to find information by association.

It is this idea—that information should be linked and searched by association—that inspired a computer scientist at CERN, the European Organization for Nuclear Research, to develop a way of finding information on the rapidly expanding Internet in the late 1980s and early 1990s. Concerned with the loss of information across numerous projects and as people come and go, Tim Berners-Lee proposed to develop the World Wide Web[22] as a means of finding information in the rapidly expanding Internet. The first version of the web and the web browser were not produced until 1991, nearly fifty years after the publication of Bush's article.

Berners-Lee was addressing a problem that was not unique to CERN and that was already an issue in using the Internet. The Internet was already fairly well established in certain sectors of academia and in certain government organizations by the late 1980s, having grown rapidly over a few years. With no efficient means of knowing what was actually available, some had already made attempts to develop ways of "indexing" the information on the Internet. These approaches differed in an important way from the Berners-Lee approach. Instead of enabling searching by association, these indexes were typically just lists of available topics.[23] The World Wide Web was designed to enable associative searching, which would mimic how people actually think, and is precisely what Vannevar Bush argued for fifty years earlier.

Although the lineage from Bush's vision to Berners-Lee's execution is clear, the solution was not, which partially explains why it took nearly fifty years to get from an idea to implementation. Both technical and conceptual challenges needed to be overcome. In fact, despite the clear lineage, Berners-Lee did not even know of Bush's article when he first created the World Wide Web.[24] But Bush's influence is unmistakable; it just happened to be transferred through some intermediaries who also happened to tackle some critical conceptual challenges that lay between vision and implementation.

The technical path from Bush to Berners-Lee follows that of the development of the computer—through the development of computer networks—to the actual Internet. Although Bush described the memex as a personal device that had the functional storage capabilities of the most advanced library with a human-friendly information-retrieval system, he never addressed how the device would be updated with the most recent information. As computer power advanced, the personal computer developed the raw storage capabilities envisioned by Bush. However, it was the development of computer networks that enabled the rapid transmission of the most recent information (as well as research collaboration) to researchers looking to advance their particular field.

The most important computer network in the second half of the twentieth century, ARPANET, was built for the military. After the Soviet Union launched *Sputnik 1* in 1957, the United States became very concerned with closing the perceived technology "gap" with its Cold War enemy. As a result, the Advanced Research Project Agency or ARPA, which has since been renamed DARPA (for Defense Advanced Research Project Agency), was established in 1958 to ensure that US military technology would remain superior to that of its enemies. DARPA is a somewhat unique agency, as it does not maintain laboratories of its own but funds and manages projects through both academic and commercial organizations.

The idea for the original ARPANET occurred in the early 1960s as the brainchild of J. C. R. Licklider who, similar to Vannevar Bush, was also a former MIT professor. Licklider's role in the ultimate development of the World Wide Web was conceptual as well as operational. From the operational standpoint, Licklider was the head of ARPA's Information Processing Techniques Office (IPTO) for two years, during which time he initiated the development of ARPANET as a means of linking the computers of the ARPA-affiliated organizations together.[25] Although it took years to develop, Licklider initiated the project and inspired his successors: Ivan Sutherland, who created the first interactive computer program, and Robert Taylor, who eventually became the director of Xerox's famous PARC research and development facility. Thus, Licklider had a direct and critical role in the development of the technological backbone of the Internet (which, as we will see, started as ARPANET) on which the World Wide Web resides. IPTO was responsible for funding numerous projects, all primarily focused on improving the functionality of computers to enhance and extend humanity's knowledge.

In addition to funding the initial projects that would grow into ARPANET, Licklider's influence on the computer industry stemmed from his desire to improve the interaction between user and computer. In his famous 1960 essay, "Man and Computer Symbiosis," Licklider articulated his vision that computers need to be designed to serve the needs of humans.[26] This both echoed and expanded on Bush's vision of the computer as an aid to human information gathering instead of as merely a general calculating machine. He also foresaw a geographically distributed network of computers. Licklider was so inspired by Vannevar Bush that his 1965 book, *Libraries of the Future*, was dedicated "however unworthy it may be, to Dr. Bush."[27]

Bush's article also inspired Douglas Englebart, the inventor of the mouse and the first graphical user interface (GUI). A GUI is the type of display that uses visual icons and graphics to enable the user to interact with the computer as compared to the traditional interfaces that required the user to interact with the computer by typing specific text "commands" into a command line. Englebart was "inspired" by Bush when he read the *LIFE* version of "As We May Think" while in the army in the Phillipines.[28] Licklider and Englebart were linked, however, by more than just their joint admiration for Dr. Bush. While director of IPTO, Licklider funded Englebart's Human Factors Research Center at the Stanford Research Institute, which is where the mouse and the GUI interface were developed. Englebart's lab also was one of the first four nodes (along with those at UCLA, UC Berkeley, and the University of Utah) linked on ARPANET in 1969, making the first electronic computer network.

Englebart also implemented the first well-known version of hypertext, a critical component of the World Wide Web. Hypertext is a vital technical innovation called for by Vannevar Bush and an important step in the development of the World Wide Web, because it enables the user to move from one piece of information to a related piece of information "on demand," allowing users to access information in the same way people think. Although Englebart did not invent hypertext (it was invented by Ted Nelson), he expanded on the idea and was the first to actually implement it, which he did at his Human Factors Research Institute. He also publicly rolled out hypertext, along with the mouse, the GUI interface, interactive video conferencing, and multimedia displays with split screens in 1968 at what has become described as one of the "most famous events in computing history."[29]

Thus, by the beginning of the 1970s, the two key requirements in the development of the World Wide Web—the distributed computer network and the hypertext approach to linking documents—had been conceived of and developed. Despite this, it took more than twenty years for the World Wide Web to develop. There are a couple reasons for this. First, although the original technologies had been developed in the late 1960s, the original versions were rudimentary. Second, the late 1980s saw an explosion in the number of computers networked together, which increased the pent-up demand for an innovative way to sift through all the available information.

The best way to highlight the dramatic increase in the magnitude of information available to ARPANET/Internet users is to look at the number of computers that had access to the Internet. From the original four-computer network in 1969, the number of computers linked to the Internet grew to approximately two thousand in 1985. This number increased exponentially over the next few years and is estimated to have reached 159,000 by late 1989.[30] This explosion in the number of computers linked to the network was less the result of expansion of Internet sites, which had already expanded to include the vast majority of universities as well as government and military sites, than the expansion of the number of computers linked to each site.

In the 1970s researchers at Xerox had created the Ethernet—a means of connecting computers that are relatively close together, such as in a single building, for the purpose of sharing printers, sending e-mail, and so forth. With the widespread adoption of personal computers in the 1980s, primarily driven by the inspiration of Apple and the business acumen and authority of IBM, the number of individuals or groups of individuals who owned computers increased dramatically. As these computers became linked over a local Ethernet at a university that already had access to the Internet, for example, there occurred a sharp spike in the number of computers that were accessing the Internet.

What these users found, however, was that they needed to know exactly what they were looking for and exactly where it was in order to actually use the Internet. Protocols had been around for years to access and transfer files across the Internet (many users over the age of thirty-five may recall the File Transfer Protocol for example), which enabled the near-instantaneous transfer of information from one location to another, but this was dependent upon knowing that this information existed and exactly how to find it. This quickly proved limiting, so numerous methods of searching through the rapidly increasing information were developed to meet the demand. The most popular of these initial "search engines" were the Wide Area Information Server (WAIS) and Gopher. Both these applications took the critical lead asked by Bush nearly fifty years earlier by enabling users to search by the content, even enabling users to search for specific words and retrieve documents that contained those words.[31]

Although these applications became popular to the relatively small group of fairly sophisticated academic and scientific users, they failed to create the dramatic surge in Internet usage that followed the development of the World Wide Web. These applications were limited by the fact that they could not handle all the different types of file transfer programs that were on the Internet (the Internet was/is an agglomeration of multiple types of networks all linked together) and, moreover, they were limited to purely text-based applications. The development of the World Wide Web by Berners-Lee resolved this final critical technical issue, although it still took years before Berners-Lee's or any other World Wide Web–based search engine had greater usage than the most popular pre-web search engine, Gopher.

As Berners-Lee put it, in the 1980s, "incompatible networks, disk formations, data formats, and character encoding schemes, which made any attempt to transfer information between dislike systems a daunting and generally impractical task,"[32] riddled the high-energy physics community. The need for a way of bridging all these different systems was particularly acute in this "community," which was an early adopter of advanced computing technology.

Berners-Lee recognized that in order to build a search engine that would truly enable users to access the full potential of the Internet, he would have to first build a system of standards on which his next-generation search engine would work. The World Wide Web included critical design features and innovations that ultimately enabled the usability of the World Wide Web to go well beyond that of the Internet on which it resides. One of the important design features of the World Wide Web was the concept that it could connect information from any source, enabling it to interact with any current system on the Internet as well as any new systems that would arrive in the future. In this way, it was designed to be completely open, flexible, and scalable.

In Berners-Lee's original proposal to his superiors at CERN in 1989, he indicated that this system needed to be both "portable, or supported on many platforms" and "extendable to new data formats."[33] Although these critical components were incorporated in the technical design of the World Wide Web, they also were incorporated into the "legal" design. The web application would be available for free to anyone, and anyone had legal rights to build upon it. This "open architecture" ultimately provided the flexibility for others to extend upon the initial web design.

In addition to the concept of "open architecture," Berners-Lee also incorporated a system of common standards for designing and referring information on the web. Berners-Lee proposed the use of a HyperText Markup Language, commonly known as HTML, as a standard approach to designing web pages. As noted before, the actual use of "hypertext" was around for more than twenty years when Berners-Lee proposed his HTML. In fact, he designed it to be very similar to the most popular hypertext language at the time—the standard generalized markup language (SGML)—in order to improve adoption.

An improved programming language was only one of the key features of the World Wide Web. Berners-Lee also defined a Universal Resource Identifier (URI) to make sure everyone was using common "language" for identifying and finding information. The most obvious URI is the HyperText Transfer Protocol (HTTP), which was designed to allow for the transfer of information between any two types of systems. Again, a standard for this had already existed at the time: the File Transfer Protocol (FTP). FTP, however, was too inflexible and too slow for the demands of the completely unconstrained web.

The development of the World Wide Web as a universal, flexible, open architecture for searching through all the available information on the Internet laid the foundation for the explosion of the web in the late 1990s. It was also a hit with

CERN users, and over the next two years it spread to other organizations engaged in high-energy physics. It did not expand much beyond that, however, and remained a relatively esoteric application among a limited academic group throughout the early 1990s. In fact, the magnitude of its future impact on the computer industry in particular and on society in general was so unobvious that a paper submitted by Berners-Lee and a colleague, Robert Cailliau, to the hypertext '91 conference on the World Wide Web was not even accepted for the conference (however, it was accepted as a poster presentation). Notably, theirs was the only presentation that dealt with the Internet that year. Within two years, nearly every presentation at the hypertext conference would relate to the Internet.[34]

One of the sites that installed the web browser software was the National Center for Supercomputing Applications (NCSA) at the University of Illinois. The NCSA was one of the original centers of the supercomputer, a concept that was becoming increasingly obsolete due to the rapid increases in personal and mainframe computing power. Looking to expand into networking to offset the decline in demand for supercomputing capabilities, a team of NCSA employees embarked on a plan to develop an improved web browser.

The team was led by Marc Andreessen, a twenty-one-year-old computer science undergraduate and a member of the computing staff at NCSA. The team developed the Mosaic web browser, which was one of dozens of web browsers that had been developed since Berners-Lee's software was launched to the world. What made this browser different was that it was much easier to install and use than most of the others, which were made by students and which failed to have the fit and finish of the Mosaic browser. The Mosaic browser was also designed for nearly any platform, from the PC, to Apples, to Unix.

Upon the release of Mosaic in November 1993, adoption was much more rapid than that of Berners-Lee's software. Within a month, more than forty thousand copies were downloaded, and within six months, an estimated one million copies were in use.[35] In a potentially ironic twist of fate, the University of Minnesota claimed ownership of Gopher in spring 1993 (presumably with the intent of selling it commercially), which potentially increased the demand for Mosaic when it was released later that same year, essentially killing the demand for Gopher as a search engine.

Although the web browser had become fairly ubiquitous, at least in many academic areas, as had an increasing number of web sites, the public was still only marginally aware of the World Wide Web. The majority of households that were using their personal computers as a tool to communicate with and find information from the external world were still using content provided by America Online (AOL) and Prodigy. The future importance of the Internet as a source of content was still opaque enough that Microsoft was in the process of developing its Microsoft Network (MSN) to be rolled out in conjunction with its Windows 95 software release. MSN was similar to AOL and Prodigy in that it was designed to be a self-contained content provider. A look at the stock price of AOL during the mid-1990s underscores the financial community's failure to see the upcoming web revolution: AOL was a Wall Street darling at that time (only to take a major fall a few years later, a common problem with "tech" companies in the nineties).

What finally put the World Wide Web into consumers' consciousness was the release of the Netscape web browser. Netscape was the first commercial web browser to have any impact—and its impact was enormous! Despite being commercial, Netscape was free to download by traditional households and consumers (revenues were derived from businesses desiring to put content on the web).[36] Netscape Communications, the company that developed the Netscape browser, originally was called the Mosaic Communications Company and was founded by Jim Clark, a legendary Silicon Valley entrepreneur who had recently sold his company, Silicon Graphics, and was looking for his next venture. Clark approached Andreessen about reproducing (and improving) what he had done at the University of Illinois, but this time as a commercial venture. Clark would provide the financial backing and Andreeson would develop the software. They originally planned to carry the brand equity of the Mosaic browser to their commercial venture, but the University of Illinois licensed the name to another company. Netscape was founded on April 4, 1994, and released its version 1.0 of the Netscape browser in December 1994. The web was here to stay.

The fight over dominance over the gateway to the information on the web has become a source of huge financial battles, not to mention the source of some of the most celebrated company successes (and failures) during the past decade. Although Microsoft already had committed to the doomed MSN, they licensed the Mosaic software and used it as the source of their Internet Explorer, which was included free of charge with Windows 98. The Netscape-versus-Explorer battle is legendary in terms of the fight for consumers, which raged for a couple years as each company rapidly launched new and improved versions to gain market share. The linking of Internet Explorer with Windows 98 also arguably pushed the Department of Justice to file its famous antitrust suit against Microsoft (the case was reminiscent of the antitrust battles between government and industry in the early days of the steel and railroad industries as well as the battles between IBM and the government in the middle of the twentieth century).

Despite the initial ruling by the Department of Justice to split Microsoft's core operating systems business from their web browser business, subsequent negotiations have left the company intact (users are now provided with multiple browser options with their Windows operating system). The net result of the "browser wars" is that Microsoft has come out victorious[37] and Netscape's share of the browser usage has dropped from more than 85 percent in the mid-1990s to less than 1 percent in 2007. Microsoft's Internet Explorer, on the other hand, now commands more than 60 percent of the web browser market.[38]

The market continues to evolve, however, as the importance of the web browser has given way to the importance of the search engine. A web browser is a software application that sits on your computer and allows users to see the pages on the Internet. The browser is the web equivalent to the operating system that allows users to run applications. Conversely, a search engine is an online tool that enables you to search and find other web sites. At the heart of the web browser is a search engine designed to help users find the information they are searching for easily and efficiently in the vast wilderness of information on the web. The number of companies that have developed approaches to efficiently find the most appropriate information is numerous, and the first company to have made a major stake in this space was Yahoo!.

Yahoo! was founded by Stanford graduate students David Filo and Jerry Wang as an extension of their own personal list service. The link to Stanford is not an accident: in addition to being one of the most competitive universities in the country, Stanford was one of the original Internet sites and has been at the forefront of the technology revolution (e.g., Silicon Valley) during the past thirty years. Stanford has become a locus for innovation. The surrounding Silicon Valley has developed an agglomeration economy in the high-tech industry that indicates the area will likely continue to lead this industry in the future. Yahoo! was originally a directory of web sites, which used more traditional hierarchical structures to categorize information, rather than a true search engine. The company ultimately evolved its capabilities (partly through acquisitions) to provide true search-engine capabilities. Ironically, from June 2000 to February 2004, Yahoo! licensed its engine from a small search-engine start-up called Google.

Google, which was also started by Stanford graduate students, was looking for a better way to identify the most appropriate information for a specific web search. The then-standard approach of ranking search results was based on the frequency that the search term appeared on the web page. Google founders Larry Page and Sergey Brin recognized that the results of the traditional search did provide a list of web pages that matched the search criteria but did not help to distinguish a "good" web page from a "bad" one. Page and Brin reasoned that a highly relevant page with a large number of relevant links is more likely to be valuable to the searcher than a highly relevant page with relatively few (or no) relevant links.[39] Using its groundbreaking approach to ranking web pages, Google has become a dominant force on the World Wide Web and one of the fastest growing companies in the country. Guiding this growth is a mission statement that would make Vannevar Bush proud: "To organize the world's information and make it universally accessible and useful."[40] In other words, a modern-day memex.

While Google seeks to organize the world's information, the other web companies that have broken out from the crowd provide a similar service: the ability to easily find what one is looking for. Amazon, for example, has made it dramatically easier to find the most appropriate book on the most esoteric of topics. Similarly, eBay has allowed customers to find even the rarest items. Facebook has grown rapidly because it allows people to easily find other people. Even YouTube is really a means of finding videos. None of these companies provides its own content (yet); rather, they each provide an efficient means to search the content of others. Although there are hundreds or thousands of other Internet companies that have a focus on selling a specific product or service—that is, content providers—it is clear that the companies that are prospering the most on the web are those that enable their customers to efficiently find whatever they are looking for.

The web revolution clearly is still in its infancy, and the evolution of this technology will continue at a rapid pace. It is estimated that about 1.5 billion of the world's 7 billion people are already using the web and that this number will double within a couple years.[41] What does the future hold? Paul Twomey, former president and CEO of Internet Corporation for Assigned Names and Numbers—the nonprofit organization responsible for the global coordination of the Internet's system of unique identifiers—says, "While the web has changed our lives, we are but on the edge of a transformative revolution which will . . . provide a mechanism for the development of new business models, previously unknown ways of connecting people and communities, new possibilities for the delivery of services, and a feedback loop for the population."[42]

For Tim Berners-Lee, the vision for the World Wide Web has not yet been achieved and society has only begun to scratch the surface of what it can do: "Today, the Web is quite effective at helping us to publish and discover documents, but the individual information elements within those documents . . . cannot be handled directly as data."[43] The inventor of the World Wide Web envisions a future where we can better understand and link the information on the web, which he calls the "Semantic Web." For Berners-Lee, the Semantic Web "isn't just about putting data on the web. It is about making links, so that a person or [a] machine can explore the web of data. With linked data, when you have some of it, you can find other, related, data."[44] He and others are still in pursuit of Bush's vision.

The development of the World Wide Web bears all the hallmarks of a revolution: it encapsulates a vision that inspires, a community of people innovating to achieve that vision, and continued innovation and expansion of the possibilities that extend beyond the original vision.

Chapter 2

THE INNOVATION PROCESS

Innovation is a process, not an event. When the process results in dramatic change, it is called a revolution. The story of the numerous innovations that led to the development of the World Wide Web and the revolution being created in its wake is presented to highlight important features of innovations that are common across all revolutions. By looking at innovations across every domain of human activity, we can clearly see the key features of this process. That is, the innovation process in business is no different than in the sciences, which is no different than the process of innovation in any human domain. The process of innovation is universal.

Looking at the universal process of innovation, we can clearly dispel the myth that innovation results from the great leaps of individuals. Innovation is a social process, not the result of some solitary genius isolated from the rest of the community. Innovations are the result of a group of people—a community—whose combined efforts lead to a novel solution. This is not to say that individuals are not critical to the innovation process. As we have clearly seen in the story of the development of the World Wide Web, certain individuals play key roles either by identifying the most important problems or by actually developing innovations that solve the most important problems.

While all innovations are the result of a social process, individuals must still do the work. But what is clear from the development of the World Wide Web as well as the dozens of other innovations that have been explored is that the innovation process for an individual is similar to that of the community. In fact, they are symbiotic—the ability for any one individual to innovate is critically dependent on the ability of that individual to interact with others, directly and/or indirectly, as he works toward a solution. This importance of social interactions is demonstrated by the stories of the printing press from six hundred years ago and the World Wide Web most recently.

To innovate successfully, both the individual and the community must progress through three key steps: first, every innovation is the result of the search for a solution to a problem; second, every innovation is the result of a reconceptualization, either to develop a unique solution to an old problem or as a reconceptualization of the problem itself; third, there is a germination phase between the problem identification and the reconceptualization that (1) can vary considerably in duration and (2) can represent the process of the individual innovator as well as that of the innovator's community.

PROBLEM IDENTIFICATION

The process of innovation has a striking similarity to the Alcoholics Anonymous's twelve-step program—to be successful, they both must start with the recognition that there is a problem. Just as an alcoholic can have a difficult time coming to this recognition, many people, organizations, industries, and governments are slow to recognize they have a problem as well. Our individual and collective ability to recognize that we have a problem runs counter to strong psychological forces that make problem recognition particularly challenging.

For many people and organizations, recognizing a problem implies that there is something wrong with the current approach. For the vast majority of us, this is very hard to accept. This is true even when faced with mountains of evidence. As psychology has increasingly challenged the decision-making process as being rational, numerous human biases have been identified. One particularly strong bias is a universal tendency to be overconfident. In a classic test of overconfidence, students were asked to spell a word and then provide their level of confidence that they spelled it correctly. When students indicated that they were 100 percent certain that they spelled the word correctly, they were correct about 80 percent of the time.[1]

Studies of entrepreneurs have also found excessive overconfidence, with entrepreneurs who are just starting out exhibiting a much greater degree of confidence than entrepreneurs who have already been successful.[2] Leading behavioral economists—a relatively new group of economists that are combining psychology and economics to better understand human judgment and decision making—have gone as far as claiming, "Perhaps the most robust finding in the psychology of judgment is that people are overconfident."[3] Ironically, this is a rather confident assertion.

But overconfidence is not our only challenge. We also have a strong desire to be right. As a result, we have a tendency to ignore or discount evidence that does not support a decision we have made as well as a strong tendency to give too much weight to evidence that supports our decision. Psychologists call this "confirmation bias," and it has been called the "most widely accepted notion of inferential error to come out of the literature on human reasoning."[4]

Furthermore, strong evidence exists (as we might expect) to show that people have a tough time accepting when they are wrong. But all is not lost, for people can learn, and overconfidence and confirmation bias can be mitigated. When people are frequently provided with feedback on the relationship between their confidence level and their actual likelihood of being correct, they learn to become much more realistic. In a rather ironic twist, the much-maligned weather forecaster actually exhibits an appropriate level of confidence. That is, when the forecaster indicates that there is "a 70 percent chance of rain," the forecaster is correct about 70 percent of the time.[5] This is the result of constant and near-immediate feedback. The feedback on how tough it actually is to successfully start a business also explains why the experienced entrepreneurs have lower levels of confidence than the budding entrepreneurs.

This feedback mechanism, though typically delayed, is critical to enabling people and organizations to reevaluate their decisions. In practice, the real challenge in the problem identification stage, however, is not the difficulty in recognizing *that* there is a problem—even the most successful individuals and companies are always looking for improvements. Rather, the challenge in the problem-identification stage is identifying *what* the real problem is. Admitting you have a problem is difficult enough, but the really hard part is figuring out the cause of the problem.

Looking at the example of the World Wide Web, we see that the problem was clearly identified as how to efficiently and effectively find information when (1) the amount of information was growing exponentially and (2) one didn't know what was available (and where it was). Berners-Lee's solution represented the culmination of a long search to develop a system that enabled users to navigate, in an intuitive, user-friendly way, the Internet wilderness, which by then housed an already massive amount of information.

The ability to appropriately identify the problem is a characteristic that separates the great scientists from the merely good scientists—as Robert Sternberg, professor of psychology at Yale, said, "What distinguished the more eminent from the less eminent scientists was not always how well they designed or executed their experiments but rather what experiments they deemed worthy of performing in the first place."[6] A similar trait can be said of great leaders: "Leadership . . . is about coping with change . . . leading an organization to constructive change begins by setting a direction."[7]

The challenge in the problem-identification stage, however, is not limited to merely "seeing" the problem. In many situations, the problem must be identified early enough to avoid potentially significant consequences. Many organizations start to get a sign that a problem exists when they see that sales are declining or that membership is down—as nearly every organization or company uses these measures as a barometer of the health of a business. When the sales are declining or when membership is down, the question becomes, why? Or, what exactly is the problem that needs to be addressed? The difficulty in these situations is that it may be too late to solve the problem.

This is the exact problem we are potentially facing with global warming. Scientific concerns about the impact of humanity on global warming have a long history, with the Nobel Prize–winning chemist, Svante Arrhenius, the first to express his concerns about the impact of carbon dioxide emissions in the late 1800s. In the 1950s, scientists began collecting atmospheric concentrations of carbon dioxide,[8] and by the early 1990s the vast majority of the scientific community came to the conclusion that global warming results primarily from the actions of humans.[9]

As a result of this delay in accepting the problem of human-induced global warming, global temperatures are projected to continue to rise for the rest of the century.[10] The challenge we face is that our ability to reduce the human impact on global warming, mainly through reduced fossil-fuel use, is hampered by a lack of politically acceptable alternatives. At the present time, the costs of alternatives to fossil-fuel use make the switch economically unbearable. Without dramatic technological innovations to make alternative energy sources economically viable, we will need innovative policies to induce all countries to accept the economic costs of switching to alternative fuels.

The acceptance of the problem of human-induced global warming has many parallels to the acceptance of a problem within a company. In an organization that is doing well, the voices that argue the product/service has important problems that need to be addressed are frequently dismissed or their concerns are minimized. Once sales actually decline, it is frequently too late for the company to fix the problem and slow the decline.

The federal government faces a similar problem with the national debt. The national debt—which is the total amount of money the government has borrowed to finance such expenses as wars, entitlement programs such as social security, and the various economic stimulus packages—has risen dramatically over the last three decades and is expected to exceed our gross domestic output this year. This is the highest ratio of debt to output since the end of World War II.[11] While economists consider borrowing as an acceptable approach to minimize economic fluctuations, excessive borrowing is a concern because lenders are worried that the borrower may not be able to pay back the money.

The concern about the federal government's level of borrowing is similar to concerns banks have when individual households or businesses want to borrow too much, and the consequences might turn out the same. When a household or business that already has borrowed a lot wants to borrow more, lenders require a greater interest rate to make up for the increased risk of default. When the cost of paying the debt becomes very high, the ability to pay that debt becomes increasingly uncertain.

Alan Greenspan[12] and many other economists have been arguing that the nation's excessive amount of debt threatens the national economy and our long-term economic performance. The US government has been unable to curtail the mounting debt as one short-term need after another has led to continued borrowing. If investors ultimately become concerned that the US government cannot pay its debt, they may stop lending and/or may require a greater rate of return. Such a move could potentially cripple the economy, requiring significant and rapid spending cuts, which would have dramatic ripple effects throughout the economy. It could lead to a sharp rise in unemployment, or even to a devaluation of the US dollar, which would be the equivalent of declaring bankruptcy for the US government. These concerns were recently expressed by the Chinese government, the largest lender to the United States, underscoring how troubling our debt level has become.

One of the largest causes of our ballooning budget, which leads to increases in the national debt, is healthcare, primarily through the ever-increasing costs of Medicare and Medicaid.[13] Healthcare costs have far outstripped inflation for the last two decades and have become a major source of concern for government and industry alike. The United States spends more on healthcare than any other nation, yet our average life expectancy is below nearly every other major industrialized nation.

Identifying the exact problem to be tackled is rather difficult. Some argue it is the health insurance companies themselves that are engaged in price gouging and in reaping excessive profits. Others argue that the pharmaceutical companies are taking advantage of our patent laws and patent protection to limit competition and reap excessive profits. Others argue that it isn't the companies that are to blame, but rather the unhealthy lifestyle of Americans as we require more healthcare throughout our lives than those in other industrialized nations.

Looking at some of the industries that are facing significant challenges today, we can see how imperative it is to correctly identify the problem. Given the concerns about spiraling health costs along with the relatively low life-expectancy rates when compared to other industrialized countries,[14] the health-care industry is facing significant pressures. The pressures on the healthcare industry have created increasing pressure on the pharmaceutical industry. The Food and Drug Administration, which is the federal organization responsible for approving new drugs, has dramatically altered its approval standards over the last few years. That has resulted in a significant drop in the number of newly approved drugs.[15] This drop, combined with the upcoming end of patent protection for some of the largest pharmaceutical products—known in the industry as the "patent cliff"—is causing profit pressures that haven't been seen in the industry for a generation. The companies are responding, as expected, by cutting costs wherever they can.

As a result, the whole sales and marketing efforts of the industry are now being questioned. Nearly every pharmaceutical company is searching for the "new commercial model" to deal with the increased profit pressures. One of the most fascinating elements of the search for this new model is how rapidly the industry has changed its opinion on the value of the traditional sales force. Despite the fact that it was well known that the vast majority of sales rep interactions with physicians have been merely "sample drops" lasting a few seconds, the industry engaged in a sales force "arms race" with the total number of pharmaceutical sales representatives numbering over 100,000 at the peak. Within just a couple years, nearly every major pharmaceutical company has reevaluated the traditional sales model and questioned the true value of the sales rep. The problem that required innovation went from "how to improve the productivity of my sales force" to "how to provide value to physicians."

These examples highlight how difficult it is to properly identify the problem. The world is complex, and it is very easy to incorrectly separate the cause from the effect. For example, depression is a common problem affecting an estimated eight out of every one hundred adults in the United States.[16] Traditionally, depression was thought of as caused by a bad childhood. More recently, scientists realized that depression is caused by an imbalance of certain chemicals in the brain.[17] Even more recently, however, it has been found that depression and the resultant chemical imbalance can result from other factors, including chronic pain.[18] While there is strong evidence that depressed people have a chemical imbalance, it is unclear whether this chemical imbalance is the cause or the effect of depression.

Mistaking cause and effect can most easily be seen in the analysis of performance in sports, where the incorrect use of statistics is rampant. There is nothing more seemingly correct but completely meaningless than the massive statistics that are thrown at you before and during a game. For example, analysts frequently compare the historical performance of two teams against each other as a sign of the likelihood of who will win the current game, despite the fact that the owners, coaches, and players are completely different. Similarly, we frequently hear the fact that the football team has won all its games when it runs the ball twenty-five times or more as evidence for the conclusion that the team should run the ball twenty-five times. There are numerous other interpretations of this data that are ignored. Of course, perhaps the passing game was so good that the other teams decided to "shut down" the pass and force the team to run. Another possibility is that the team ran the ball more often after getting a lead in order to run out the clock. In both cases, it could be the success of the passing game that creates the success of the running game.

Similarly, we hear in hockey that the team wins all its games when it gets more than fifty shots on goal. Getting a lot of shots on goal is typically a sign that the team is outplaying the other team and getting good opportunities. If the team started taking every shot, even from far distances, just to get fifty shots, I can assure you that the statistic would no longer hold. In baseball we might hear something like "the team wins 80 percent of its games when the players hit two home runs or more." Well, given that home runs create runs, and winning requires having more runs than the other team, this is basically saying the team wins 80 percent of their games when they score a lot of runs!

We use these sports examples to illustrate how an improper use of statistics can mask the ability to properly distinguish cause from effect, which is a frequent challenge to correctly identifying a problem. But, when used correctly, statistics can help identify not only the problem but also the solution. Ironically, baseball has gone through a revolution in recent years due to an innovation in the way statistics are being used. Above all other major sports, baseball is and has always been a sport of statistics. As documented in *Moneyball* by Michael Lewis, people began to challenge whether the traditional statistics, such batting average and earned run average, were properly measuring the value of the player to the team's performance.[19] The result has been a revolution in the statistical evaluation of players that has led to a more efficient evaluation of player value.

While the baseball example underscores how difficult it is to identify *what* the real problem is (why the teams with the biggest payrolls are frequently outperformed by teams with smaller payrolls) it also highlights an additional challenge to the problem-identification stage: consensus. This is most evident in the debate on global warming. While the vast majority of scientists believe the statistics support the theory of human-induced global warming, there are some well-respected scientists who do not accept this theory. Similarly, while the majority of economists believe carrying a large national debt is detrimental to long-term growth, there are many well-respected economists who disagree. This is the same in nearly every industry and organization, where a consensus opinion will form regarding the true problem to be addressed.

While it is assumed that the consensus opinion is based on the best reading of the facts/statistics, there is plenty of evidence that popular opinion can at times be very, very wrong. The popular eighteenth-century book *Extraordinary Popular Delusions and the Madness of Crowds* highlights numerous examples of a failure of the popular opinion.[20] More recently, Alan Greenspan famously identified the "irrational exuberance" of the stock market prior to the dot-com crash,[21] and Nobel Prize–winning economist Robert Schiller published a popular book that identified a dramatic weakening in mortgage-lending standards that fueled the rapid acceleration in housing market prices prior to the mortgage crisis.[22] Despite these influential voices, based on strong statistical evidence, the consensus opinion failed to recognize the problem until too late.

As these examples illustrate, gaining a consensus that there *is* a problem and a consensus of *what* the problem is can be very difficult. But both are critical to getting to a solution. While there is always a certain degree of tolerance for nonconsensus opinions, the vast majority of research—and funding for research—focuses on the problems identified by the consensus as most important.

GERMINATION

In between the recognition of a problem and the reconceptualizing of the available information that forms the solution is a germination process. This is the process of sifting through information, trying alternative formulations, and testing hypotheses until a solution is found. At the simplest level, the germination process is the thought process that a person goes through when trying to solve a problem. Most studies of creativity focus exclusively on the individual germination process.[23] It is important to understand the individual germination process, and we will provide a novel description of how the creative process works that enables someone to both generate novel potential solutions and select an approach from the infinite possible solutions that will likely work. However, it is the germination process of the community that is critical to obtaining a solution. The biggest difficulty in the germination phase is the inability to accurately assess just how long this phase will last. While for some problems this phase could literally last only a couple days, for many problems this phase can extend across many generations. For most problems, the length of the germination phase is strongly related to the size of the community working on the problem. This underscores the importance of the group's "consensus" correctly identifying the problem.

The picture we have of the germination phase of the World Wide Web looks very different if we look at it from the perspective of Tim Berners-Lee than if we look at it from that of the "information retrieval" community. For Berners-Lee, the germination phase lasted nearly a decade, as he first tackled the problem of information retrieval at CERN in the early 1980s and retackled it when he came back in the late 1980s. If we take the broader community view, then we see that the germination process for the World Wide Web took about half a century: it started with Vannevar Bush postulating a way of organizing and sorting through the rapidly expanding volumes of information, and it culminated with the marriage of the Internet and hypertext that Berners-Lee named the World Wide Web.

The World Wide Web case study illustrates that the germination phase can be very long, and moreover, it shows that it can be very difficult, if not impossible, to quantify how long this process will take. In contrast to Moore's law, where computing power was correctly predicted to double every four years,[24] we have a Fermat's Last Theorem example. In the middle of the seventeenth century, the French mathematician Pierre de Fermat scribbled a note in the margin of a notebook indicating that he had developed a proof for a vexing problem related to the Pythagorean theorem (though he didn't provide the proof). Partly inspired by Fermat's confidence, this proof was considered to be on the cusp of being solved . . . for the next 350 years!

The good news is that for some well-defined problems, there are clearly defined experiments/tests of a proposed solution. We will see that Einstein not only proposed a novel theory but also proposed tests that could be performed that could either support or refute his theory. While a theory can never be proven, and it can only become strengthened, some have argued that what separates good theories from bad theories is that good theories can be proven false.[25] Among the biggest critiques against astrology and even many forms of Eastern medicine is that they cannot be tested to be proven false. Interestingly, some have made this exact charge against some of the most highly regarded scientific theories, most notably the theory of evolution, as well as against many theories in the social sciences. The use of controlled experiments to test the specific impact of a single variable provides a very powerful means of testing proposed solutions. The bad news is that it may be very difficult, or even impossible, to actually perform the test. Even worse, it is not clear how many different hypotheses will need to be tested before finding the correct solution.

In regard to human-induced global warming, the problem has become fairly well defined—our atmosphere is trapping a greater amount of the sun's heat due to excessive greenhouse gas emissions, which is causing a global increase in average temperatures. Since the problem is broadly defined, the range of potential solutions being explored is vast and creative. We are clearly in the middle of the germination stage as numerous scientists, economists, and politicians are exploring ways to reduce the rise in global temperatures. While most approaches focus on reducing the emission of greenhouse gasses, primarily through a reduction in fossil-fuel use, some approaches have focused on ways to remove the greenhouse gasses from the atmosphere.

The push to reduce emission from automobiles is the most pronounced example of the first approach—that of reducing our emissions of greenhouse gasses. With the automobile representing the most significant source of greenhouse gas emissions, a dramatic reduction in automobile emissions represents one of fastest paths to greenhouse gas reduction. Impressively, there are numerous approaches to reducing automobile emissions that are already making it to market. In addition to the popular hybrid vehicles, which use a regular gas engine combined with a regenerative battery system, some automakers are focusing on clean diesel technology, which is surprisingly effective. In addition, others are exploring plug-in electric technology. The Chevy Volt, perhaps the most anticipated American car in a generation, and the Nissan Leaf are just two examples of the plug-in electric approach. Both cars use an extensive battery system that gets recharged by using a standard household outlet (the Volt also includes a backup gasoline engine). This approach creates dramatic gains in fuel efficiency. Other, less well-known examples exist, including the exploration of solar, biofuel, and hydrogen-powered cars.

While these technologies have made a splash in the first decade of the new millennium, the germination phase for many of these technologies goes back to the 1970s when the US economy was nearly crippled by the skyrocketing price of oil. Consequently, the US government invested hundreds of millions of dollars into alternative technologies aimed at reducing our demand for foreign oil.[26] Since the "problem" was reducing our dependence on expensive foreign oil—not reducing our greenhouse gas emissions—the decline in oil prices in the 1980s led to a dramatic reduction in government-funded research into alternative energy sources. As a result, the germination phase for solving the problem of reducing our greenhouse gas emissions was effectively delayed.

There are ways to potentially reduce the length and uncertainty of the germination phase, but they come with tradeoffs. The length of the germination phase, in general, will vary based on the number of people working on solving the problem as well as the size and difficulty of the problem. In addition to having more people work on the problem, which typically requires a greater degree of consensus or "buy-in," an effective way to potentially reduce the length of the germination phase is to narrow the search for a solution to those approaches that show the most initial promise.

This is arguably the most common approach to problem solving, as it is the instinctive approach people take to most problems. Numerous experiments have shown that when faced with a problem, people will explore the path that shows the most initial success. This has been called "hill climbing" and it been shown to be a highly efficient approach to solving many problems using computers.[27] Although this approach is frequently the most efficient, there are times when it can be very inefficient and will fail to find the solution even when one exists. The hill-climbing approach is very efficient because it identifies the most effective initial approach and follows that "path." The hill-climbing approach becomes very inefficient if that path proves to be a "dead end," because it is very difficult for a person to recognize whether he has merely hit an obstacle or whether he has hit a dead end. At this point, the problem solver must go back to some previous point and look at alternatives. The question becomes, how far back should he go?

RECONCEPTUALIZATION

Just as every innovation begins with identifying a problem, the culmination of every problem-solving process is a reconceptualization. That is, regardless of whether someone is working on an abstract math problem or is trying to devise an improved automobile engine, the solution is always conceptual. The actual solution may involve numerous physical tests, but the solution begins with an idea as to which specific test to run and why. In the popular view of innovation, the reconceptualization is that flash of insight that most people think of when they imagine the "eureka" moment.

The reconceptualization is best illustrated by a visual analogy. There is a famous picture that looks like a vase from one reference point and looks like a pair of faces looking at each other from another reference point. The information contained in the picture doesn't change, but the interpretation of the picture changes from one reference point to the next. Switching from one image to another requires a reconceptualization of the picture. This is exactly what happens when a solution is found—a reconceptualization of the available information enables the problem to be solved.

In most cases, the reconceptualization involves developing and interpreting new information in a novel manner. In some cases, the reconceptualization may lead to a restatement of the problem itself. We will see in the next chapter that a reconceptualization of the problem itself often leads to more dramatic revolutions, which can open up a much larger set of possibilities to be explored. If we look at the World Wide Web revolution, we can see that Berners-Lee reconceptualized the challenge of linking computers on the Internet and the challenge of providing a flexible approach to finding information on a computer as being part of the same problem. He thus saw the need for a universal approach to linking and finding information. In the next chapter, we will see how Einstein reconceptualized our basic definition of space itself. By allowing space to "curve," he was able to reconcile some fundamental issues that had been challenging physicists since Newton developed his theories two hundred years earlier. Later on, we will see how the American Revolution was sparked by a reconceptualization of the source of political power. The founders of the American Revolution were bolstered by the enticing theory of inalienable human rights and were able realize that a hereditary monarchy was fundamentally inconsistent with equal rights.

Looking at some of the industries that are going through revolutions today, we can see the reconceptualizations that took place to spark those revolutions in the first place. In keeping with the sports theme earlier, the National Football League has been going through a revolution since the 1970s as a result of the introduction of the West Coast Offense. The West Coast Offense is credited as being developed by Bill Walsh in the early 1970s while he was at the Cincinnati Bengals, and it was implemented in the 1980s with the San Francisco 49ers, leading the 49ers to three Super Bowls.[28] The West Coast Offense reconceptualized the role of the pass to the offense. The traditional view was that a good running game was critical to the success of the offense, as passing came with much greater risks, like interceptions and sacks. As a result, the traditional offense was based on a strong running attack that would be augmented by the pass. By establishing highly efficient, quick-release plays, the passing game no longer needed to be considered higher risk (and therefore more appropriate for situations where the offense needed the higher reward) than the running game. The system has evolved since, but it has been adopted by nearly every team in the league in some form over the past twenty years.

After nearly one hundred years, the electric utility industry is undergoing a reconceptualization of its own that is leading to a complete restructuring of the industry. Traditionally, the electricity industry has been considered a natural monopoly.[29] That is, since a house or business needs only one electricity provider and since the costs required to attach electricity wires from a generation station to every house and business are extremely high, the first firm to establish the initial wires will have a monopoly over its customers (since switching costs will be too high). The government, therefore, took over the regulation of the electric utility industry in the early twentieth century and has maintained regulation ever since.

Originally, the power plant that generated electricity was directly connected to the homes and businesses it served. This system would consist of the power plant, a set of transmission lines that carried large volumes of electricity, and a set of distribution lines that would carry a small portion of the electricity from the transmission line to the specific household or business. Under this system, loss of a single transmission line or generation plant would leave every house and business served by that power plant without power. To solve this problem, the electric utility industry developed a system of interconnected systems with redundant transmission lines that enabled the power created from a generation plant to be able to service a house or business in a different region. This system limited the disruption typically known as blackouts, like the famous blackout in New York City in 1977, or brownouts, which cause power loss to subsets of customers when the demand exceeds peak capacity.

Since electricity follows the path of least resistance, the

interconnected systems and redundant transmission lines made it technically impossible to determine whether the electricity a household or business receives is generated from a distant or local power plan. This really didn't represent a problem at first since the utility companies still knew how much electricity they produced and how much was used by the local households and businesses. The utilities would pay each other for differences in production and local consumption.

In the 1990s, government officials realized that due to the interconnectedness of the utility industry's transmission system, the traditional end-to-end natural monopoly no longer existed. While it was true that the owner of the line that runs into the house or business would still have a natural monopoly over that customer, the specific power generated for that house was no longer a natural monopoly. In the beginning, the power generator was directly linked via transmission and distribution lines to the customer in a closed system. As each system linked to each other, the owner of the generator no longer had a natural monopoly on the customer.

Officials reconceptualized the electric utility industry into two industries, one that delivers power to customers, which was still a natural monopoly, and one that generates electricity, which would now operate in a competitive market. Over the past twenty years, the industry has been slowly evolving closer to this new paradigm. The process will continue for a couple more decades as the decision of when and how to deregulate is done at the state level and as the legislatures wrestle with the challenging issue of "stranded costs." Since generators are very expensive to build, regulators would approve the building of a new power generator and would guarantee that the costs to build the plant would be recovered, typically over thirty years. However, stranded costs are those costs that were approved under the old system but would be lost in a competitive environment (the costs to build power generators have varied considerably, which partially explains why electricity prices vary so much across the country).

Going back to the healthcare industry, we see that the industry is also going through a revolution due to a reconceptualization of the role of the physician in the treatment decision. Historically, the local physician was considered the best authority on how to treat his patient. The initial reconceptualization started with the health insurance companies, who switched from insurance companies that base their fees on actuarial tables to managed-care companies that focus on controlling costs.

These managed-care organizations have reconceptualized their role as being active participants in the treatment decision. While their original approach was to negotiate for lower costs, the reconceptualization has led them to require authorization for certain procedures as well as the use of copay and reimbursement schedules to actually influence the treatment decision. For example, in many classes of prescription drugs there are numerous products with a similar mechanism of action. Managed-care companies have doctors on staff to decide whether these products are substitutes and, if so, may decide to set different patient copay rates for these similar products. One product may require a patient copay of five dollars while another product may require a patient copay of twenty-five dollars. While the doctor and the patient still have the final decision as to which product to use, the change in the cost to the patient can have a dramatic effect on which product is chosen.

The reconceptualization process is the culmination of a long journey that involves both the individual and the community searching to identify and then solve a particular problem.

For individuals and organizations looking for the next break-through, getting a clear description of the problem is critical. Just as writing one's goals down has been shown to increase the odds of achieving the goal, writing the problem down serves as a critical reminder of a tangible goal and forces a precision in thought that may not occur otherwise.

We've seen throughout this chapter the risks associated with problem solving. In particular, the path from problem identification to solution is usually circuitous, and solutions frequently come from unlikely paths. We clearly saw this in the circuitous development of the World Wide Web. When embarking on a program of innovation, the organization must recognize the time and costs that may be required as well as recognize that a solution is not guaranteed. There is inherent risk in the innovation process. In addition, it is clear that individuals and organizations must be willing to embrace alternative approaches, even some that may seem ridiculous, in order to find the best solution. The best solution can frequently be overlooked or ignored because it flies in the face of conventional wisdom.

The next chapter provides a story of two reconceptualizations that required a complete rejection of the status quo, leading to a fundamental shift in humankind's view of the universe. We will see how difficult accepting such a reconceptualization can be, even for the most brilliant minds. Managers and business leaders looking for innovation must be prepared to reject the status quo and must be willing to accept a solution that contradicts current beliefs. In subsequent chapters we will look at ways to improve the likelihood of finding the solution to a problem, and we will also lay out the process that an innovation must go through to lead to a revolution.

Chapter 3

THE RELATIVITY
REVOLUTION

On October 24, 1927, the most exclusive club in the world met at the luxurious Hotel Britannique in Brussels. The Britannique stands in the city center as the pinnacle of luxury. However, at that time it was infamous for being the headquarters for the German Kaiser during the occupation of Belgium in World War I. On this cool fall day, twenty-three of the most gifted scientists in the world convened for the sixth Solvay science conference.[1] Of these handpicked participants, sixteen were former or future Nobel Prize winners.[2] If there ever was an intellectual dream team, this was it.

The purpose of the meeting was fitting for such a crowd, it was to discuss recent advances in quantum theory and the theory of radiation.[3] While the conference included presentations by a handful of the luminaries, the real action is reported to have occurred in the discussions over breakfast and dinner. It was during these times that the most famous debates in modern science occurred. These debates were between Albert Einstein, the 1921 winner of the Nobel Prize in physics, and Niels Bohr, the 1922 winner of the Nobel Prize in physics, over the proper interpretation of the results of quantum theory.[4]

Although both men were larger than life, Einstein was unquestionably considered the leading physicist of the time. He not only created the theory of relativity, a theory univer-

sally respected for its beauty and its far-reaching consequences, but he was also one of the founders of the quantum
theory. But Bohr and Einstein had very different views of the
proper interpretation of quantum theory, with Bohr's representing the most vocal proponent of the "Copenhagen interpretation" of quantum mechanics that had been developed
over the previous year.[5] This interpretation argued that nature
was fundamentally probabilistic, not deterministic. This interpretation struck at the foundation of the interpretation of all of
science, which has always assumed the world is driven by
cause and effect.

The debates started each morning at breakfast, where Einstein would pose challenges, usually in the style of thought
experiments, to Bohr's interpretation. Each night at dinner,
Bohr would provide his response to those challenges, frequently in detailed mathematical form. Although little is
known about the exact nature of these discussions outside of
this general pattern, firsthand accounts of these discussions
indicate that Bohr exposed Einstein during these debates as a
scientific conservative who was clinging to prejudices from an
earlier time.[6] In the years following this conference, Einstein
continued to challenge the Copenhagen interpretation even as
he recognized that his view represented a smaller and smaller
minority in the physics community.[7]

The twentieth century saw the toppling of numerous regimes—
political, ideological, and scientific. Perhaps the most significant of all was the complete overthrow of humankind's view of
the universe. Our view of the universe was generated in the seventeenth century by Sir Isaac Newton, arguably the most influen-

tial thinker and scientist in the Western world. Although Newton developed calculus and made significant advancements in the theory of optics, his most important and enduring work was the *Principia*, which laid out the laws of motion and gravity and the nature of space.[8] Newton's work did not merely dominate the physics community for the next two hundred years, but it actually represented the foundation on which all advancements in physics came to be based.

The overthrow of the Newtonian system by Albert Einstein's relativity is both fascinating and illustrative of the key themes detailed in the previous chapter. The physics community was clearly facing a problem due to a series of failed tests of a fundamental theory in Newton's system. There was a long germination phase as numerous attempts to explain the failure were postulated. In what is considered the most impressive insight in modern times, the theory of relativity reconceptualized the foundation of physics. This reconceptualization led to an ongoing revolution in physics that continues to this day. This revolution also highlights some other key features typical of many revolutions, such as the importance of new information, how revolutions in seemingly distinct areas can ultimately become connected, and how revolutionaries—even the most brilliant ones—can quickly become conservatives.

The overthrow of Newtonian science, which culminated with the publication of Einstein's theory of general relativity in 1915, began over seventy-five years earlier in eastern Europe in a seemingly unrelated field. In the middle of the 1800s, a revolution occurred in the field of geometry, a field that had been more stable than any other for the last two thousand years. Up until the middle of the 1800s, geometry, as laid out by Euclid in 300 BCE, was generally considered the pinnacle of scientific thought[9]—it had been continuously expanded and used successfully for thousands of years. Scientists, philosophers, and mathematicians looked to develop all fields of inquiry using the approach mastered by Euclid in his development of geometry. This approach emphasizes deductive logic over inductive logic. In deductive logic, we start with some minimal assumptions and develop proofs for conclusions that cannot be refuted. The following is a famous example of deductive logic:

> All men are mortal.
> Socrates is a man.
> Therefore:
> Socrates is mortal.

In this example, if we agree that the first two statements are true, then we have to agree that the conclusion—"Socrates is mortal"—is true. Based on logical arguments of this type, Euclidean geometry was developed and expanded from its creation in ancient Greece up through the 1800s. This method also had a strong influence on the development of science throughout this time.

Despite the reverence for Euclidian geometry, there were some "technicalities" in Euclid's geometry that bothered mathematicians for thousands of years. It is not that they didn't believe in the truth of Euclidean geometry; rather, they felt that one of the assumptions was too strong and just needed to be proven. In order to understand the problem, we need to first discuss how Euclid built his geometry. Euclidian geometry starts with a series of twenty-three basic definitions, five postulates, and five common notions. Examples of the definitions, which are assumed to be true, include the definition of a point and a straight line. These definitions—along with the postulates and common notions—are considered to be uncontroversial, although they are also not provable. From this simple foundation, mathematicians have been developing a complex series of geometrical proofs.

While mathematicians have generally accepted Euclid's framework, they struggled with one assumption—the so-called parallel postulate. The parallel postulate is the definition of parallel lines that we are all familiar with from basic geometry. That is, if we have a straight line and a point not on that straight line, there is a *single* straight line that will pass through the point that will *never* cross the original straight line. The problem mathematicians had with the parallel postulate was not that it was false, for they believed it to be true,[10] but rather that it required the additional assumption about an infinitely long line. Many mathematicians felt that it was inappropriate to just assume that infinitely long lines never meet. They felt this needed to be proven.

To the mathematicians the problem was clear enough—prove the parallel postulate. Yet, in this case, the germination phase was very, very long. While numerous attempts to prove the parallel postulate were made over the years by the most notable mathematicians, and some of those proofs were even thought to be successful for extended periods of time, mathematicians failed to develop a proof for the parallel postulate for thousands of years. In the early 1800s, János Bolyai was another in a long line of mathematicians who felt he could solve the problem of the parallel postulate. When he learned of his son János's quest, Farkas Bolyai, himself a distinguished mathematician who unsuccessfully tried to prove the parallel postulate, counseled his son against trying to prove the parallel postulate, as it would only lead to failure and frustration: "You must not attempt this approach to parallels. I know this way to its very end. I have traversed this bottomless night, which extinguished all light and joy of my life. . . . I turned back when I saw that no man can reach the bottom of this night. I turned back unconsoled, pitying myself and all mankind."[11] Although this is clearly hyperbole, it does highlight the difficulty of János's undertaking.

János started his approach by assuming the parallel postulate was false, which was actually a well-worn path. The goal of this approach was to prove that this assumption would ultimately lead to a logical contradiction in geometry. Since everything else in the deductive proof is true, the contradiction would actually serve to prove the postulate in mathematical sense. This is also the approach that had vexed the smartest mathematical minds for millennia. Instead of finding only darkness, however, János found success—although it was not what he first expected. While János expected to use the assumption that the parallel postulate was false to lead to an inconsistency in Euclidean geometry, János instead found that by ignoring the parallel postulate altogether, he could create a completely new geometrical system that was just as valid as Euclidean geometry.

This was not a complete rejection of Euclidean geometry, but it was a rejection of the assumption that the parallel postulate was necessarily true. That is, Euclidean geometry lost its role as *the* geometry and became *a* geometry. As an aside, when secondary-school teachers speak of geometry today, they are still referring only to Euclidean geometry, despite the fact that there are numerous known geometries. I can remember the degree of consternation I personally felt when I learned that Euclidean geometry was known to be just one of many possible geometries.

This finding was immediately recognized as having potentially far-reaching consequences for mathematics and to the nature of space itself. In fact, it wasn't long before this discovery that Carl Friedrich Gauss, one of the greatest mathematicians of all time, wrote an extremely prescient letter to a friend discussing his concerns about Euclidean geometry: "I come more and more to the necessity that our geometry cannot be proved. . . . Perhaps we shall come to another insight in another life into the nature of space, which is unattainable for us now."[12] Gauss's foresight is impressive both in his ability to see that other geometries are possible and in his ability to see that our conception of space itself would then be called into question—which is exactly what relativity ultimately did a century later. The significance of this discovery was not lost on the elder Bolyai, as Farkas showed a degree of insight regarding the nature of such monumental discoveries when he counseled his son that "no time be lost in making it public. . . . there is some truth in this, that many things have an epoch, in which they are found in several places."[13]

Farkas's remarks are also particularly prescient, as Nikolai Lobachevsky, a mathematician unknown to the Bolyais, came to the same conclusion at nearly the same time. For two mathematicians—who had no direct connection—to solve a two-thousand-year-old problem at the same time highlights a common theme of innovation: even the most profound innovations and discoveries happen by multiple people at about the same time. This reinforces the notion that innovations are social phenomena, for it is the communication of new ideas and developments across the whole community—either through direct conversation or through publications—that lead individuals to make discoveries. There are numerous other famous examples where groundbreaking innovations occurred nearly simultaneously. For example, we earlier referred to Newton as the inventor of calculus. Well, the actual inventor of calculus is not exactly clear, as Gottfried Leibniz independently invented calculus at about the same time (with a famous subsequent dispute over who could lay claim to being the actual inventor). Similarly, Charles Darwin hurriedly published his theory of evolution once he learned that his friend Alfred Russel Wallace was about to publish the same theory.[14]

Despite the continued advancement of non-Euclidean geometry throughout the rest of the nineteenth century and the recognition by those working in the field that these advancements called into question the true nature of space, physicists scarcely knew about these developments. The true implications of the "downfall" of non-Euclidean geometry were not realized until decades later and not until a crisis emerged in physics that challenged our understanding of both space and time.

The dominant notion of space and time in the late nineteenth century derived from Newton's theories developed at the end of the seventeenth century. At the heart of Newton's "system" was the law of gravity, which explained how objects influence each other based on their mass and their distance from each other, and a view of both space and time as absolute and independent of any observer. The law of gravity was a huge success from an experimental standpoint, as it explained a vast amount of phenomena that couldn't be explained before, but was significantly questioned from a theoretical standpoint. The notion that objects influence one another "from a distance" was challenged by many of Newton's contemporaries, and Newton himself disavowed this explanation as he asserted that he didn't understand exactly how gravity worked.[15]

Since scientists were not comfortable with the idea that objects could influence each other without directly touching (or by touching an intermediary), they speculated that space was filled with something called *the ether*. For example, the ether explained how the light from the sun could travel through space to reach the earth, as it was thought that the light traveled "on" the ether. The ether was basically described as an invisible, ever-present, superlight gas. It is not that they didn't believe the ether existed; they just needed to prove it. The search for the ether became an ongoing experimental problem for physicists. For hundreds of years scientists repeatedly looked for, but couldn't detect the ether. Finally, a growing concern became a "crisis" when, in 1904, an experiment that was universally believed to be sufficiently powerful to detect the ether failed to find any trace of this mysterious substance.[16] In a strikingly similar pattern to the "fall" of Euclidean geometry that resulted from the failure to prove the parallel postulate, the "fall" of Newton's physics resulted from the failure to prove the existence of the ether. (This is not to say that Newton's physics have completely fallen from grace. In most situations we'll ever encounter, Newton's equations are accurate.)

In the case of this experiment, scientists were trying to measure the impact of the ether on the speed of objects (light in particular) and had devised ingenious experiments to detect this mysterious substance. In particular, the results failed to show any influence of the ether on the speed of light. To understand the issue, we can imagine throwing a ball on a moving train. If you throw the ball in the same direction as the train, the speed of the ball will be found to be equal to the speed of the train plus the speed of the thrown ball. This simple additive calculation was fundamental to Newton's physics and has been verified numerous times by scientists. However, if someone shines a flashlight on a moving train (or, more appropriately turned on an oil lamp in the mid-nineteenth century), the speed of light would NOT equal the speed of the train plus the speed of the light. That is, the speed of light doesn't change, regardless of whether it is shown on a moving train or on the train platform (to keep the metaphor). Scientists noted that the speed of light, for some unknown reason, always came out the same regardless of how fast its source was moving.

The failure to detect the ether as well as the finding that the speed of light never changed ran completely contrary to the classical Newtonian physics. The crisis transformed the problem itself. Instead of trying to find and measure the ether, physicists tried to explain how light could move without the ether to carry it. This new problem opened the doors for creative solutions to what had become an increasingly troubling result. At first, scientists looked for a way to explain these seemingly inconsistent results while maintaining the status quo of Newton's highly successful system. This is a common feature of the germination phase, as the bias is to find a solution that is most consistent with the status quo. Within months, H. A. Lorentz, the chairman of that fateful 1927 Solvay Conference on Quantum Mechanics, developed a set of "transformations" that preserved the Newton calculations by allowing bodies to change size based on their speed. That is, the faster something was moving, the shorter it became.[17]

While this was a novel concept, it did not violate any of the basic principles of the Newtonian world. However, the approach made additional assumptions that, when viewed differently, were unnecessarily complicated. The willingness to accept greater complexity is also a common approach to solutions that are biased toward maintaining the status quo. This bias can help us understand why incumbents in an area are less likely to explore truly novel solutions. Those who are well entrenched within a system or wedded to a product are biased toward solving the next problem with that particular system or product in mind. This is part of the reason why products become increasingly complex, as uses for a product continue to be expanded. While in many situations this may be the most effective approach, it can also lead to unnecessary complexity and inefficient solutions to newer problems.

With a newly minted doctorate, the young Albert Einstein was relatively less entrenched with the status quo and was willing to let go of the unnecessary complexity. Shortly after Lorentz published his results, Einstein proposed an alternative view of how to interpret the available information. In his groundbreaking paper "On the Electrodynamics of Moving Bodies," published in 1905, Einstein accepted as true that the speed of light is constant and that objects *appear* to contract as they move faster, and he concluded that *time itself was relative*.[18] This conclusion struck at the heart of Newton's conception of absolute time and led to some amazing results. Despite the groundbreaking result, Einstein recognized that his efforts were a reconceptualization of the available information: "The special theory of relativity . . . has considerably reduced the number of independent hypotheses forming the basis of [this] theory. The special theory of relativity has rendered the Maxwell-Lorentz theory so plausible, that the latter would have been generally accepted by physicists."[19] Einstein also argued that if he didn't show that time is relative, someone else soon would have.

The implications of the "special theory of relativity" were dramatic. For example, by showing that the speed of an object was a function of the mass of the object, Einstein then derived his most famous equation: $E = mc^2$ (energy equals mass times the speed of light squared). From this equation, as speeds approach the speed of light, the energy required approaches infinity. This equation also leads to the law of conservation of matter and energy, which states that matter and energy are equivalent and the total amount of matter and energy in the universe is constant. While the implications of the special theory of relativity were far ranging, Einstein himself pointed out that "the special theory of relativity does not depart from classical mechanics through the postulate of relativity, but through the postulate of the constancy of the velocity of light"[20] from which all of the other implications were derived. Thus, a simple reconceptualization of single idea caused a complete overhaul of a historically highly validated system.

One important area that had not been overhauled was the nature of space itself. As Einstein explained: "The modification to which the special theory of relativity has subjected the theory of space and time is indeed far-reaching, but one important point has remained unaffected . . . the laws of geometry."[21] Ironically, in a letter reminiscent of the senior Bolyai imploring his son not to tackle the problem of the parallel lines, Einstein's friend Max Planck, himself a Nobel Prize winner and founder of quantum physics, implored the young Einstein not to try to tackle gravity: "As an older friend I must advise you against it for in the first place you will not succeed; and even if you succeed, no one will believe you."[22]

Despite this warning, Einstein pursued the integration of space and gravity with the new theory of time. The problem Einstein (and others) now faced was clear: how could light, which was always found to move in a straight line, be "bent" by gravity? The solution—general relativity—resulted from over a decade of work by Einstein and numerous other physicists. Einstein again solved this problem by a reconceptualization, this time of the nature of space itself.

Similar to his approach to solving the problem of special relativity, Einstein again started by accepting the seemingly contradictory evidence—that light moves in a straight line *and* that light appears to be "bent" by gravity—as both true. As Einstein showed, these can both be true in a non-Euclidean geometry. That light moves in a straight line seems exceptionally trite at first blush, until we realize that Einstein is defining straight as the shortest distance between two points. In our day-to-day life, the shortest distance between two lines is clearly "straight" in the traditional sense. This is the space of Euclidean geometry. However, in non-Euclidean geometries the shortest distance is not "straight" in the traditional sense. For example, the shortest distance between two points on a sphere such as a basketball is not "straight" in the traditional sense.

How can light move in both a straight line and a curved line at the same time? It merely depends on where you are standing—Einstein used the concept of the "frame of reference" (which he also used to explain the special theory of relativity) to explain how. If you are "standing" on the light as it travels across the basketball, it will look like you are going straight. However, if you were looking at the light from above the basketball, the light would appear to bend. Einstein realized that gravity did not "act at a distance," but rather objects moved through "bent" space. That is, by assuming that light always took the shortest path, Einstein reconceptualized our notion of space and did away with the traditional view of the "spooky action at a distance" concept of gravity. Thus, the reason that a ball thrown up into the air comes down is because "down" reflects the path of the curvature of space. (Technically, it is a straight line in four-dimensional space-time.)

In a particularly telling insight into a fundamental challenge faced throughout the innovation process, Einstein described how he had solved the core problem required for general relativity seven years before the theory was finalized. He asked rhetorically, "Why were another seven years required for the construction of the general theory of relativity?"[23] He answered that he had to "free" himself from certain traditional "ideas" about the nature of space. The ability to let go of traditional ideas partially explains why the theory of relativity was not discovered sooner and also explains why Einstein became marginalized during the next revolution in physics. The power of experience and assumptions is one of the strongest forces that hamper both innovation and the ability to adopt an innovation, even for the most brilliant.

In the first years of the twentieth century, the French mathematician-turned-physicist Henri Poincaré recognized, just as Einstein did over fifteen years later, that absolute space was unnecessary and that space could actually be non-Euclidean. But Poincaré explicitly rejected that physicists would be willing to accept non-Euclidean space and would rather assume that light does not move in a straight line. In a rather fateful display of confidence, Poincaré claimed that "Euclidean geometry . . . has nothing to fear from fresh experiments."[24] Poincaré even used the term "relativity" when discussing whether space was Euclidean or non-Euclidean: "The law of the phenomena which will be produced in this system . . . this is what we will call, for the sake of brevity, the law of relativity."[25] That Poincaré was so close to recognizing the full impact of relativity but rejected the notion of non-Euclidean geometry underscores how important assumptions can be. That Poincaré was so close to the theory of relativity itself (along with H. A. Lorentz) reinforces the notion that innovation is a social phenomena, as we again see how other members of the community were very close to identifying the theory of relativity.

How the theory of relativity came to be accepted by the physics community also helps to explode the myth that the superior "product" always wins. The fact was that the theory of relativity had little empirical support to indicate it was superior to Newtonian physics, but the theory was highly regarded anyway. Despite the limited empirical support, many scientists were drawn to it because of its "beauty."

For example, Ernest Rutherford, one of the greatest experimental physicists of the twentieth century and the 1908 Nobel Prize winner in chemistry, spoke for more than one physicist when he claimed that the "theory of relativity by Einstein, apart from any question of its validity, cannot but be regarded as a magnificent work of art."[26] Wolfgang Pauli, himself a Nobel Prize winner for his work on quantum mechanics, described Einstein's theoretical feat this way: "This fusion of two previously quite disconnected subjects—metric and gravitation—must be considered as the most beautiful achievement of the general theory of relativity." [27] Similarly, Paul Dirac, also a Nobel Prize winner for his work on atomic theory, described Einstein's achievement: "There was difficulty reconciling the Newtonian theory of gravitation with its instantaneous propagation of forces with the requirements of special relativity; and Einstein working on this difficulty was led to a generalization of his relativity—which was probably the greatest scientific discovery that was ever made." [28]

Despite the view by many empirical and theoretical physicists that Einstein's general theory of relativity was "beautiful," it was not initially clear whether the theory was simpler than the traditional view of space or if it predicted actual events better, or both. It is often considered that Einstein made three "predictions" in his paper that enabled physicists to empirically compare the performance of the general theory of relativity against Newtonian physics.

The third and most famous prediction was that the light from other stars would appear bent due to the gravitational pull of the sun. While it would not be possible to detect such a shift under normal conditions due to the interference of the light coming from our sun, a solar eclipse would provide the opportunity to test whether light was in fact bent by the sun. The first chance to test this prediction occurred in 1919 and was taken up by the astronomer Sir Arthur Eddington, who was director of the Cambridge Observatory and the leading astronomer of his time. In 1920, Eddington famously published his "Report on the Relativity Theory of Gravitation," concluding that Einstein's theory was validated by the results.[29]

As other physicists evaluated the data, however, many questioned whether the data actually supported Einstein's theory any better than Newton's theory. As late as 1958, Werner Heisenberg, of the Heisenberg uncertainty principle fame and one of the leaders of the next great scientific revolution—quantum physics—claimed that "whether the deflection agrees quantitatively with the value predicted by Einstein's theory has not yet been decided."[30] The problem was due to insufficiently precise instruments. It wasn't until the 1960s that the physics community gained sufficient empirical evidence to confirm Einstein's prediction.

In the early 1920s, physicists were faced with a unique challenge—accept the "beautiful" theory of general relativity with its limited empirical support or continue to work on the well-supported, yet limited Newtonian physics. As the next generation of physicists arose—those who grew up on the new theories of relativity and quantum physics—while the older generation was retiring, the general theory of relativity became more and more mainstream in the physics community.

As a result of the relative lack of evidence, as well as a considerable number of doubters within the physics community, Einstein's Nobel Prize was granted "for his services to Theoretical Physics, and especially for his discovery of the law of the photoelectric effect."[31] Thus, it was Einstein's work on the foundations of quantum physics, not his work on relativity, that earned him the Nobel Prize. Einstein's work on the photoelectric effect showed that light, which was well known to move in waves, *also* moved as singular particles.[32] This dual nature of light became a cornerstone of quantum physics.[33] Notably, Einstein's paper on the particle nature of light was published in 1905, the same year as his principle of special relativity.

Ironically, it was Einstein's work on the dual nature of light that led to the reintroduction of "spooky action at a distance," a Newtonian concept recently rejected by Einstein. The physics community struggled to explain how some experiments showed that light was composed of individual particles while other experiments showed that light acted as a wave. Almost two decades after Einstein's photoelectric results, Neils Bohr argued that these two views of light—acting as a particle and as a wave—were "complementary" pictures of the same reality.[34]

Further exploration of quantum effects, especially the Heisenberg uncertainty principle, led to the radical conclusion—embodied in the Copenhagen Interpretation—that the action of light was probabilistic in nature. This is what led Einstein to famously claim that "God does not play dice with the Universe."[35] Einstein's considerable success was based, in part, on his experience that whenever he encountered something that could not be explained, the failure was always due to our lack of knowledge. As a result, Einstein steadfastly refused to accept that this interpretation of quantum physics was complete. As the vast majority of physicists came to accept this view, Einstein became an increasingly isolated voice.

The Copenhagen Interpretation was "finalized" by the spring of 1927, only months before the infamous Solvay conference in which the view of Einstein as being out of touch with the physics community began to emerge (even Einstein recognized that his views were considered reactionary by others). While his utter rejection of a probabilistic universe is well known, it is less recognized that Einstein had a fundamental assumption that causality required a direct physical link. By reconceptualizing space, Einstein was able to abolish the notion of action-at-a-distance implied in Newton's theory of gravity. In what has become his most cited article ever,[36] Einstein and two other physicists published a paper in 1936 challenging the probabilistic nature of quantum theory on the grounds that it implied that either particles moved faster than the speed of light or action-at-a-distance actually existed.

Neils Bohr, Einstein's nemesis at the Solvay conference, was extremely concerned with the implication of this paper, as he believed that if the argument is correct, then this would lead to a complete collapse of quantum physics itself.[37] In response, Bohr quickly published a reply arguing that the assumptions were invalid. Ironically, thirty years later, the topic was taken up again by a physicist at CERN, the future home of Tim Berners-Lee, who showed that the "spooky action at a distance" was a fundamental part of quantum physics.[38]

As technologies have developed to enable physicists to peer further into the universe and create energies hitherto unheard of from manmade machines, Einstein's theories have not only been validated to exceptional degrees of precision, but they have begun to bear additional fruit as the implications of these theories are more fully understood. For example, the idea of a "black hole," a space so full of mass that light could never escape, is a direct result of Einstein's general theory of relativity. In addition, the most celebrated physicist of our time, Steven Hawking, has used Einstein's theories to show that the universe must be dynamic and that it had to have had a beginning (e.g., the "big bang").

In what Einstein later called his own most significant blunder, Einstein introduced a "cosmological constant" into the equations of his general theory to ensure that the universe was static. Similar to Euclid's assumption about the parallel postulate and Newton's assumption about absolute space, this constant was recognized by others as basically unnecessary. Dropping this assumption required a reconceptualization of the universe itself, as the results then implied that the universe was not static. This reconceptualization was supported by Edwin Hubble in the 1920s when he recognized that the light from distant galaxies had a different color (it was redder) than the light from nearby galaxies, implying that the light emitted from these galaxies is moving away from us.

Einstein's impact goes well beyond the physics of stars, galaxies, and the universe, as his notion of the interconnectedness of all of physics and his reconceptualization of space and time into relative terms has redefined how scientists think about their own work. In the words of Heisenberg in the late 1950s: "Though the experimental basis of general relativity is still rather narrow, the theory contains the ideas of the greatest importance. . . . In the theory of general relativity these questions about the infinity of space and time can be asked and partly answered on an empirical basis."[39]

Despite these glowing remarks, the exact role that the theory of general relativity plays in physics is still being worked out. It has been known since it was first proposed that it is inconsistent with quantum physics. Einstein spent the last years of his life trying to reconcile these two inconsistent frameworks. Perhaps the greatest challenge to theoretical physicists today is finding a theory that will reconcile these two highly validated yet seemingly inconsistent theories.

Chapter 4

THE NATURE OF INNOVATION

At the core of innovation lies a paradox—while an innovation is evolutionary, the effect can be revolutionary. This is the fundamental duality of innovation. To understand this duality, we must recognize that the nature of an innovation can look fundamentally different depending upon your "frame of reference." An individual's frame of reference—which Einstein used in developing both the special and general theory of relativity—is an important concept that enables us to understand the mystery of innovation itself.

The two primary case studies we've discussed thus far illustrate how innovations fundamentally alter our view of the world; moreover, they appear to those not immersed in the community as revolutionary leaps forward. However, as we have seen in these same cases, a close inspection of the development of each innovation represents, to those immersed in the field, an evolutionary extension of the then-current thinking. This leads to the duality of innovation: while an innovation is itself evolutionary, the effects can be revolutionary.

For example, despite the great and well-deserved praise for the brilliance of the theory of general relativity, the theory clearly represents an extension of the ideas of the time. While Einstein did put all the relevant pieces together into a coherent whole, which is a considerable intellectual achievement, even the great Einstein was standing on the shoulders of others. As we have seen, it was immediately recognized that the development of non-Euclidean geometry meant that the true nature of space needed to be redefined by scientists nearly one hundred years before Einstein reconceptualized space as relative. Similarly, while the World Wide Web has revolutionized information sharing, the Internet and hypertext were already developed by the early 1990s. Furthermore, there was a long history of researchers seeking a means to effectively search through a rapidly increasing amount of information. Quite simply, Berners-Lee was able to develop an efficient information retrieval system for the Internet, a purely evolutionary innovation. Again, while this extension required great expertise and insight, it also represented an extension of the ideas of the time.

Also supporting the evolutionary view of innovation is the frequency with which innovations have occurred at nearly the same time by more than one person. We have already discussed a few examples, including the famous battle between Newton and Leibniz over who invented calculus and the independent development of non-Euclidean geometry by both János Bolyai and Nikolai Lobachevsky. The example of how Darwin quickly published his theory of evolution to preempt Alfred Russel Wallace highlights a subtlety regarding multiple versions of the same innovation: in most cases the publication by the first innovator stops the search process by others. That is, "redundant" innovations only happen when the results of the first innovator are unavailable to others who are pursuing the same innovation. As the speed at which innovations are communicated has increased, the likelihood of a redundant innovation has decreased.

The examples of dual innovations underscore how important it is to be the first to solve the problem. Being first clearly has its perks—from the recognition itself to the financial benefits of the first-mover advantage and to patent protection. While the first to market an innovation is not always the most successful, the advantages are considerable in terms of recognition.

The question that must be answered is, why did that particular person (or organization) develop that particular innovation at that particular time? Understanding the factors that lead to innovations will enable us to create the proper conditions for innovation, which is critical to reducing the time to innovation. Looking across a broad range of disciplines—from the arts to the sciences, to politics, and even to competitive games such as chess—we will explore the three catalysts to increase innovation and dispel some deeply ingrained myths of innovation.

FROM MOTIVATION TO INSPIRATION

Motivation represents the most obvious and most paradoxical catalyst of innovation. A look at the lives of the most successful artists, scientists, athletes, politicians, and businesspeople illustrates the importance of motivation. In order to achieve the pinnacle of any domain, innate abilities are not sufficient—one must be motivated. We all know of individuals from our youth who had great natural talents but failed to achieve eminence because they lacked the necessary motivation. The significance of motivation in achieving success is obvious in any endeavor, and particularly in endeavors that require creativity. Everyone understands that developing innovative solutions to challenging problems is difficult and requires a highly motivated individual who is willing to work hard and for long periods of time without clear success or, frequently, without clear progress.

The paradox of motivation is that it is critical to innovation, yet most attempts at motivating people to be innovative are actually counterproductive. That is, most attempts to motivate a person or a team to solve a problem will actually decrease the likelihood of a successful solution. This is the paradox that has developed around the idea of extrinsic motivation. Extrinsic motivation refers to any attempt to increase motivation that comes from an external source, such as from a boss, a teacher, or a parent. This is in contrast to intrinsic motivation, which is the internal desire to solve a problem.

Many studies of creativity have shown that creative output is reduced when the subjects know their output will be evaluated. The evaluation is an external motivator. The subjects tend to be less creative as their thought processes seem to be limited by the desire to develop solutions that they think will be considered creative rather than find the solution they think is best. The psychological community has found so much support for the importance of intrinsic motivation over extrinsic motivation that they have developed the "intrinsic motivation principle of creativity," which postulates that intrinsic motivation is always conducive to creativity while extrinsic motivation is almost always a hindrance to creativity.[1] In fact, the support for this is considered so strong that "this proposition has been elevated to the status of an undisputed principle."[2]

With experience as a guide, overconfidence seems to set the stage for a reconceptualization. When something is undisputed (which sounds eerily familiar to the confidence supporting Euclidean geometry and the absolute nature of space as well as the confidence in the interpretation of quantum theory), it is often a sign that the idea, or product, is incomplete (if not downright wrong). But how can this undisputed principle be wrong? Let's first look at some examples of extrinsic motivation that surely seem to be successful.

The importance of external motivation is clear in the numerous uses of competitions to spur solutions to problems requiring innovative solutions. In these examples, a competition is established—which is clearly an external motivator—in order to spur innovation and enhance understanding in a particular field. One famous example is the computer prisoner's dilemma tournament set up by Robert Axelrod to evaluate the best evolutionary competitive strategies. The goal of the tournament was to evaluate the best strategy for when to cooperate and when to defect, when faced with the famous prisoner's dilemma. In this competition, as in the prisoner's dilemma, the greatest reward is given if you defect while the other player cooperates. The lowest reward is given if both players defect. Axelrod put out an open call for the submission of computer programs that would describe the actions taken when they were paired up with each of the other programs. Axelrod actually held two different competitions, neither of which included any compensation, with the first drawing fourteen competitors and the second drawing sixty-two competitors.[3] Despite no financial incentives and the external motivator of the competition, the results were highly successful and were reported in the journal *Science* as well in the popular book *The Evolution of Cooperation*.

In 1996, the Ansari X Prize competition was announced. This competition put out a ten-million-dollar "carrot" for any nongovernmental organization that could send a manned ship beyond the atmosphere and bring it back successfully twice within two weeks.[4] A total of twenty-six teams entered the competition, and after eight years and many failed attempts, the company Scaled Composites, which was backed by financial support from Microsoft cofounder Paul Allen, successfully won the prize and captured the attention of the nation. The competition was inspired by the Orteig Prize, which was offered in the early twentieth century to the first person to fly nonstop from New York to Paris. We have all seen a picture or short video clip of the winner, Charles Lindbergh, getting out of his plane and celebrating the historic event.

The X Prize Foundation clearly believes in the power of extrinsic motivation to foster innovation. It states: "The mission of the X Prize Foundation is to bring about radical breakthroughs for the benefit of humanity. We do this by creating and managing prizes that drive innovators to solve some of the greatest challenges facing the world today."[5] The power of the prize is reiterated by the conclusions drawn by McKinsey and Company, arguably the most prestigious management consulting company in the world, about the value of competitions and prizes: "Prizes attract diverse groups of experts, practitioners, and laypeople—regardless of formal credentials—to attempt to solve difficult problems, dramatically expanding the pool of potential solvers, and lower the cost of attempting or recognizing solutions."[6]

In each of these examples, a "carrot" was offered to motivate people to develop innovative solutions to difficult problems. The importance of the "carrot" to performance can clearly be seen in the well-known effect of a "contract year" in professional sports. While not directly a measure of creativity (although creativity likely increases), higher performance is frequently seen when incentives are applied in professional sports such as baseball, basketball, football, and hockey. In these sports, athletes typically sign multiyear contracts with their teams. It has been well documented that a player's performance frequently improves in the final year of his contract.[7] It is generally considered that this effect is the result of the player's being more motivated to put in extra effort in that year order to position himself for a much more lucrative contract the next time around.

The business world is full of examples of external motivation—with no more glaring examples than stock options and bonuses. The use of stock options is particularly prevalent in young firms as a tool to provide incentives to employees to work, innovate, and help the company grow (for these small firms, options also provide greater potential return to compensate for greater risks). The annual bonus is designed to maximize the productivity of employees. For those employees in product development, innovation is an essential part of productivity. Thus, the bonus is clearly designed as an external motivator.

Finally, and a bit ironically, the use of the "carrot" is rampant in academia. In order to obtain a doctorate, one must expand the knowledge (i.e., innovate) of a particular field. The process is known to be both very difficult and (sometimes) extremely tedious, yet many people are willing to spend years on this challenging task. Moreover, in order to become a professor, one must publish a large number of innovative, peer-reviewed articles. The high weight placed on innovation in academia means either that these external motivators are actually hurting our educational system or that it is serving as a powerful motivator.

How do we explain the apparent contradiction between the "undisputed principle" known as the intrinsic motivation principle of creativity and the frequent and very successful use of incentives to inspire improved performance and greater creativity? Can both be true? The simple answer is yes. The paradox is resolved when we recognize that intrinsic motivation is not generated independently of the outside world. People are social animals, and our intrinsic motivation is influenced by our social goals. Psychology has identified a near-universal desire that merges both forms of motivation—the desire for recognition. This need can be described as one of pride—in a negative sense—but it has repeatedly been characterized as a basic human desire.[8] The "carrots" that have been discussed are all examples of symbols of success, which tap into our underlying need to be recognized.

The use of external motivators, then, can be highly effective when they tap into this powerful human desire. This is not to say that a particular external motivator will have the same effect on everyone. The symbol of success is not the same for everyone: for some it could be money, for others it could be fame, while for others it could be simple recognition. Whatever the symbol, an appropriate external motivator must be able to tap into the individual's intrinsic motivator and provide an opportunity where he or she can achieve the symbol of success.

Also, of supreme importance, the appropriate external motivator must be implemented correctly. The problem with incorrectly implemented external motivators is that they can be perceived as coercive.[9] The critical feature of an external motivator is the individual's freedom to choose to participate. For all the "carrots" we discussed, the participant had the option to participate or not. While most if not all the participants in the competitions described above would not have tackled those specific challenges without the rewards, they still had the choice of whether or not to participate.

This represents a considerable challenge for managers since most employees do not have the freedom to choose what they want to work on. Consequently, the delegation of tasks can be *demotivating*. The addition of management guidelines, such as timelines and specific approaches, can make the task even more demotivating. This represents a fundamental problem to management—how to motivate employees when they do not have the freedom to choose their task? It is simply not possible to let most employees choose their own tasks and run a successful organization. It is possible, however, to make sure the task is delegated while giving the employee as much freedom as possible. For example, though the specific goal of the task may not be flexible, the manager can ameliorate the perceived "coercion" by providing as much freedom as possible about *how* to hit the goal. This approach provides the employee with the freedom to choose the approach, preserving the perception of choice. Of course, this is not always an option, and the possibility of providing the freedom of how to achieve the goal is greater for those tasks that do not have a prescribed solution. Whenever both motivation and innovation are required, managers should give the employee a specific objective but not dictate a specific approach to meeting the objective.

The good news is that there are two reasons why intrinsic motivation can be high even when the employee is provided with specific tasks with specific solutions to those tasks. First, employees recognize that they have control over their fate—they accepted the job and they can quit at any time. This preserves the sense of control, which is critical to intrinsic motivation. Of course, if the job is very different than originally presented and/or the employee is realistically unable to quit, then the employee will no longer feel able to choose, so intrinsic motivation will suffer. There are numerous reasons why employees cannot just quit, from the simple fact that they need to find another job first to their not wanting to be perceived as "job hoppers," to their needing end-of-year bonuses to pay off debt. Managers must always be on the lookout for employees who feel "trapped" for these reasons, because their motivation and ultimately their contributions to innovation will almost certainly be low.

Second, and most important, there is another universal motivating force that managers can tap into to increase intrinsic motivation—the need for meaning. Viktor E. Frankl famously discussed man's search for meaning as one of the driving forces in our life.[10] This meaning can be found by being a part of something "bigger." The ability to help someone see how his job, however menial, is part of something much bigger than himself can offset many of the demotivators that are inherent in the workplace. This is what separates managers from leaders. Leaders provide their followers with a sense of meaning that is bigger than the individual. That is, true leaders inspire, and inspiration is the greatest form of motivation.

History has clearly shown the power of inspiration. John F. Kennedy famously implored Americans to "ask not what your country can do for you, ask what you can do for your country."[11] Ronald Reagan was described as "the great communicator" because he was able to convey a vision of the country that inspired millions. Barack Obama inspired Americans with the simple slogan of "yes we can." While political leaders represent the most dramatic case of inspiration (and sometimes the reverse), the ability to inspire is not restricted to politicians. The greatest CEOs are those who lead by inspiration.

There are many great CEOs, but perhaps the one most notable for inspiring an innovative company is Steve Jobs of Apple. Jobs is legendary in Silicon Valley as a visionary who, during two separate reigns as CEO of Apple, has shown an ability to create passion in his employees as well as in his customers. In addition to inspiring innovation, Jobs is famous for his ability to convey a sense among his employees that they are a part of a cause larger than themselves. This was most apparent when he lured the then-president of PepsiCo, John Sculley, with the infamous line, "Do you want to spend the rest of your life selling sugared water to children, or do you want a chance to change the world?"[12] Needless to say, Sculley joined Apple.

The ability to inspire others is not limited to those at the top of the organization, although the scope of their influence is undeniable. The most effective managers are those who can inspire their employees regardless of where they are in the organization, and the most effective organizations have inspiring leaders at every level.

THE KNOWLEDGE HORSESHOE

The importance of motivation partially explains the second critical catalyst to successful innovators—deep and diverse knowledge. In order to gain this knowledge base in the first place, a certain amount of motivation must be present. In attempting to explain creative output, psychologists have continuously reiterated the importance of achieving a vast amount of knowledge and experience. One might say that chess represents an ideal testing ground for the importance of knowledge and expertise because it has clear rules and measures of success, yet it has such a high degree of complexity that there is no single formula for success. In the research on expertise, the chess player has become the psychologist's equivalent to the *Drosophila melanogaster* (a.k.a., the fruit fly) for the biologist. The first studies on chess and problem solving were performed back in the 1940s by the Dutch psychologist Adriaan de Groot, resulting in some startling conclusions about the differences between chess experts and chess novices.

In the original experiments, chess Grandmasters and strong "club" players were both asked to talk through their thought processes when deciding on which move to make. The surprising conclusion from these studies was that there was no difference in the amount of searching between the Grandmasters and the other players.[13] That is, the better players did not differ in their ability to "think ahead," which contradicted the then-conventional wisdom of what separated the best players from the merely strong players. A crucial difference was found, however, between the two groups in their relative ability to recall briefly seen chess positions. When presented with a chessboard for a few seconds then asked to reconstruct the board, the Grandmasters were able to reconstruct much more of the board than the weaker players.

In the mid-1960s, a similar study was performed, but with an interesting twist. In this study both groups were again briefly shown chessboards and asked to reconstruct what they saw. In this study, however, some of the chessboards had pieces that were randomly placed on the board while the placement of the pieces on the other boards reflected actual game situations (similar to the original studies). While the difference in recall between the experts and novices were significant when the chessboards reflected actual gamelike positions, the differences in position recall between the experts and the novices disappeared when the pieces were randomly distributed throughout the board.[14]

These results highlighted how important experience is to performance and led to a new theory on how people store information, called "chunking."[15] This theory argues that with increased experience, a person starts to see patterns that become encoded in the brain as a single "chunk" instead of as separate elements. One of the conclusions of this theory is that it explains why experts can recall more information than novices.

To understand how this works, we will focus on the task of recalling. The ability to recall information just presented to us is known as short-term memory. Numerous studies have indicated that the normal human is able to recall about seven items from a list, such as random words. The chess studies with randomly assigned pieces indicated that the short-term recall levels were the same for the experts and the novices. When patterns in the information can be detected, however, mental chunking allows the total information that can be recalled to increase. This is because the pattern, not each item that makes up the pattern, only takes up one of the seven items that we can recall. Since the expert is more likely to recognize patterns, the expert will be able to recall more information. Thus, when the chessboard was set up with familiar patterns, the recall of the experts was much higher than the recall of the novices.

A simple test of this theory can be done by looking at the following letters for ten seconds and trying to recall as many as you can:

xehplbdygctzajefodlbbneodaysxeyped

If you are like most people, you can probably recall five to nine letters. Now, look at the next row of letters for ten seconds and see how many you can recall:

iwillrecommendthisbooktoallmyfriends

If you are like most people, you will be able to recall all thirty-six letters. This is because the letters make words—that is, letter "chunks"—and you are an "expert" on words.

The theory of chunking tells us that experts can effectively process more new information than novices (at least in short-term memory). The theory also indicates that experts are better able to recognize pattern nuances. The ability to identify slight deviations from expected patterns is critical to properly identifying problems within information, which, as we have already argued, is the most critical step in the innovation process. These implications are consistent with the notion that expertise is important to innovation. The significance of expertise is heightened, however, when we understand how the process of natural selection can explain much of the differences in creative output.

At about the same time as the theory of "chunking" was developed, Donald T. Campbell, a professor at Northwestern University, argued that the development and proliferation of creative output follows a process essentially equivalent to the natural selection process in biology.[16] Over the years, the natural selection analogy has been developed and expanded, especially by Dean Simonton of the University of California–Davis, to provide deep and compelling insights into how to foster innovation—a must for every manager and leader in every organization.

The value of this approach is in its ability to explain the considerable variation in both quantity and quality of creative output with a few fairly uncontroversial assumptions (just like geometrical proofs). The first assumption is that each person in any particular field contains a partial sample of all available knowledge.[17] This is uncontroversial as it is quite obvious that any person could learn only a fraction of the available knowledge. In fact, the problem of too much information was the inspiration for the World Wide Web. Except for narrowly defined situations, like how to win in tic-tac-toe, the amount of information available is well beyond what any one person can grasp. Even in games that have clear rules, the complexity can overwhelm even the best and the brightest. In chess, for example, even the best Grandmasters know only a small fraction of the available openings that have been observed and, when preparing for a tournament, will study a relatively small number of these openings.[18]

The second assumption is equally innocuous: the amount of knowledge is distributed unevenly across those people who participate in that field.[19] The distribution of knowledge can be due to motivation, intelligence, or even simple random chance (or all the above). One could argue that the distribution of knowledge in a specific domain actually reflects the distribution of intelligence in that domain. Given the importance of motivation and other factors, however, we would expect the distribution of knowledge to be related to both intelligence and motivation.

With these two basic assumptions, the natural selection process can explain the differences in creative output and provide guidance on how to increase the likelihood of hitting upon an innovation. The first step in the natural selection process is *random variation*. In biology, the variation is due to a pairing of individual genes to create novel combinations. In creativity, specific facts and ideas represent the "genes" and are randomly combined. The combination process creates additional and novel ideas. The combination process does not even have to be intentional. That is, each fact and idea can be randomly combined with every other fact and idea to create a new idea. Also, the new idea does not have to be good; in fact, it can be absurd. The power of natural selection is that it will weed out the absurd combinations through their inability to provide additional insight into a problem.

Through the power of combinations, a slight amount of new knowledge leads to a dramatic increase in new combinations. That is, as the amount of basic facts and ideas grows, the possible combination of basic facts and ideas grows much faster! This has important implications in regard to creative potential and can explain the diversity we see in creative output (as well as in performance in just about any domain). Let's start by assuming that the amount of knowledge of basic facts, perhaps as measured by IQ, is distributed normally throughout a population. When we look at the distribution in the number of combinations that result from those basic facts, we will get a highly skewed distribution. Those with the most facts will have exponentially more combinations of facts. Thus, the most knowledgeable person has exponentially more possible combinations than the second most knowledgeable person despite there being only the slightest difference in the number of facts they posses. Quite simply, as the amount of knowledge grows linearly, the number of possible combinations of that knowledge grows exponentially.

If the natural selection view of knowledge holds for creativity, we would expect that innovations throughout the population will be highly skewed with relatively few individuals accounting for a disproportionately large share of the innovations. This is exactly what we see when we look at the distribution of two measures of innovation—patents and peer-reviewed articles. In both cases a small number of individuals account for a disproportionately large share of the output. In fact, the distribution is perfectly consistent with the simple model where knowledge is distributed normally (i.e., the "bell" curve). The variation in creative output is consistent with variations in productivity in other areas, such as business performance. The business world has the 80/20 rule, which states that "80 percent of sales come from 20 percent of the salespeople" or, more broadly, "80 percent of the value of a company is generated by 20 percent of the employees." The distribution of peer-reviewed and cited papers follows a similar distribution.

These results have important implications for businesses attempting to focus on improving creativity and on increasing the number of innovative products (or processes). Given the well-known maxim that the best predictor of future performance is past performance, the simplest and most direct implication is that companies should hire those who have developed the largest knowledge base in the relevant subject and should provide the right incentives, and then they will benefit from a plethora of creative output. The company's job will be merely to determine which innovations are actually valuable and which ones aren't.

If it were only that simple. The first challenge is to develop a way of measuring the total amount of knowledge each person actually has obtained. In those areas where patents or publications are common, one could look at the volume of patents or publications received as a proxy for knowledge. For those who are relatively junior in their field, there will be little difference in the number of patents or publications. Given these limitations, it is reasonable to focus on the "quality" of a person's past experience when a "quantity" measure is lacking. For example, many companies focus on the "quality" of the school from which the applicant graduated or the "quality" of the firms the applicant has worked for as a proxy for future success. This approach assumes that those who come from the best schools or best companies, or who have achieved eminence at other firms, are more likely to have a large knowledge base (or a high degree of motivation—or both) than others.

Still, the notion of the lone genius is generally unsupported in the research on creativity and is underscored in each of our case studies. For example, the vast majority of publications and inventions have multiple authors, and this is increasing as each discipline gets even more complex. Moreover, as we have seen with the World Wide Web and relativity, even those innovations that are attributed to a lone individual typically reflect multiple advancements made within the field. So the innovator is aptly classified as standing on the shoulders of his community, both past and present. The challenge, then, is not to just identify the best individuals but to build the right team.

Given the exponential power of knowledge described above and its ability to explain innovation, the starting point for developing the most innovative group is to develop the most knowledgeable group. But building the most knowledgeable group is not the same as building a group full of the most knowledgeable individuals. This is because there will be a large amount of knowledge that is duplicated. Total knowledge in a group is the total *nonduplicated* knowledge. Since knowledge duplication will reduce total group knowledge, the implication is that greater group creativity will consist of members with heterogeneous knowledge. Since knowledge can be acquired from multiple sources, this implies heterogeneity in education background as well as in experience. Research on group creativity has supported this assertion, at least up to a point.

When people with divergent academic backgrounds and experiences are brought together to form a group, creativity is increased as long as they all have a minimum amount of knowledge overlap. Some overlap is necessary for communication. That is, innovation increases as diversity increases up to a point. But as diversity increases beyond that point, innovation actually has been shown to go down.[20] Putting groups together with extremely diverse academic training and/or work experience is like putting people with different languages together: they spend so much time translating that the amount of time solving problems can be greatly reduced. However, a healthy mix of individuals with diverse academic and work backgrounds can stimulate thought and innovation.

This horseshoe, or inverted U shape, also explains the surprising relationship we see between the amount of knowledge and the degree of innovation for both individuals and groups. It is clear that in order to innovate in an area, a minimum level of knowledge of the subject is necessary. Ironically, there is evidence that spending too much time gathering a deeper and deeper understanding of a small field can actually hamper the ability to be creative—too much knowledge can actually decrease creativity. (Thus, despite the compelling notion that the total amount of knowledge can explain the large diversity through the simple power of knowledge combination, the natural selection view of innovation needs some further clarification.) To understand why too much knowledge can actually lead to a decrease in innovation, we must go back to the theory of "chunking" discussed above. When too much knowledge is obtained and a high-degree of "chunking" occurs, there is an increased likelihood that incongruous information will be overlooked. It isn't that the incongruous information isn't noticed but rather that it is ignored altogether as irrelevant or is considered to be an outlier—meaningless "noise" in the data.

This helps explain why a disproportionate number of major innovations occur by relative novices in a field instead of by the most experienced members, which is readily apparent in our case studies described previously. Einstein, for example, had only recently received his doctorate when he made his first advancements in relativity. This was true of both Lobachevsky and Bolyai for geometry. In fact, they were all counseled against their endeavors by colleagues with much greater knowledge and experience. Those who have achieved a sufficient degree of knowledge but have not built too many assumptions and experience with the "accepted" rules are less likely to ignore the incongruous information. The fact is that most of the incongruous information is noise, and the more experienced person is completely justified in ignoring it. This explains why junior researchers tend to be much less efficient than their more seasoned counterparts—they spend too much time exploring the noise. The experienced researcher, however, has been down that path and has learned to see the chunks in the data, enabling him to efficiently separate the noise from the truly useful information—normally. Every once in a while, the noise actually reflects a new pattern. It is during these times that the seasoned researcher is at a disadvantage since he is more likely to assume the new pattern is just more noise. The history of innovations highlights how many of the most dramatic innovations also tend to come from a reconceptualization of this noise.

The insights into the importance of the total knowledge base of a group leads to some significant conclusions about how to maintain creative groups. In particular, innovative groups require a source of new information. Without a source of new information, the total knowledge base of the group will be "used up" after a while. The combinations with the most potential will be explored and the group will come to jointly accept certain assumptions and interpretations (chunks) unquestioningly. Consequently, if group knowledge remains constant, then the innovative output will slow down. There are, of course, two ways that a group can obtain new knowledge: additional training and member turnover (assuming the group size is constant). While both are viable, the rate of knowledge addition is much greater when different members are added than when individuals receive additional training (either on their own or through explicit programs).

There is a limit to this, as too much turnover leads to a decrease in innovation as the loss of institutional knowledge and the transition costs of absorbing and getting adjusted to new members overwhelm the gains due to the influx of new ideas. The familiar U-shaped pattern emerges here as well. This has been confirmed by research exploring group creativity. Researchers have found that innovation actually increases when there is turnover in the group—up to a point.[21]

Actively managing turnover can be both difficult and unpleasant, especially in the corporate environment, but there are other options to increase the amount of group innovation. As already mentioned, the other way to increase group knowledge is to increase the knowledge base of the individuals within the group. While the rate of knowledge acquisition typically slows as one advances in an organization, typically due to the fact that the individual must spend increasing amounts of time using the knowledge already gained instead of acquiring new knowledge,[22] there are numerous strategies for increasing knowledge and, by the transitive property, innovation. The most obvious approach is to offer continued education opportunities. Most companies have already adopted this mechanism, through formal continuing-education programs and through relevant conferences. The risk of using these programs is that they produce an increasingly knowledgeable worker who is more valuable to other employers. This is the reason most companies also require the employee to stay for a minimum amount of time beyond the completion of the advanced degree. This increases the likelihood that the company will obtain a return from its investment.

Another approach is to have employees work on multiple, diverse projects at once. Numerous studies of the most innovative and creative people show that they are frequently working on multiple projects at once. The most creative individuals have two to four projects under way at once. Working on multiple projects provides both cross-fertilization opportunities across projects, even when they are only loosely related, as well as an opportunity to put aside a project that has hit a sticking point. (Perhaps the most common approach to promote innovation is developing cross-functional task forces designed to solve a particular problem.) Another example is the development of innovation labs. An innovation lab is a separate group within an organization where employees from different parts of the organization come together to cross-fertilize ideas then return back to their original departments.

Given the pivotal role of learning new information in the innovation process, every organization should have explicit plans to maximize learning opportunities. The drawback is that acquiring new knowledge incurs costs. If the organization is facing very tight financial pressures, then it will likely curtail the spending on new knowledge acquisition. While this makes sense in the short-term, it can risk the long-term health of the company. Knowledge management is critical to the long-term health of the company and should be a part of every leader's plans.

THE CULT OF PERSONALITY

The final leg in the innovation tripod is having a personality suited for the uncertainties of innovation. This is traditionally thought of as a willingness to take risks and is most closely associated with the business entrepreneur, who is willing to forego a nearly certain financial gain for the possibility of much greater financial gain. While the business entrepreneur is arguably among the most celebrated group of innovators, innovators exist in every domain. In addition, most innovators and many entrepreneurs do not consider themselves to be risk takers at all.[23]

To understand where risk taking fits into innovation, we need to go to the leading approach to understanding personality differences. Over the past two decades, the academic community has generally agreed that differences in personality can be explained fairly well by a handful of personality traits. The so-called Big Five personality traits have been used to explain individual differences across numerous topics, including career choice, task performance, and creativity. The Big Five theory can be described by the acronym OCEAN and consists of the following five traits:

Openness to Experience: The degree to which a person is broad-minded and curious.

Conscientiousness: The degree to which a person is hardworking, responsible, and thorough.

Extraversion: The degree to which a person is outgoing and sociable.

Agreeableness: The degree to which a person is cooperative, forgiving, and generous.

Neuroticism: The degree to which a person is inhibited, moody, and concerned.

The power of Big Five theory is due, in part, to the fact that it can be measured through a relatively simple survey. This has allowed psychologists to measure individual differences and empirically test how well these measured differences explain different behaviors and outcomes. When researchers have looked at differences in innovation, they have been able to show that the Big Five helps identify which personality types are more innovative.

While innovation is actually best explained by a combination of Big Five factors, scoring high on the openness to experience trait is a good predictor of an individual's innovativeness.[24] This makes intuitive sense, since being too rigid in one's opinions and beliefs will reduce the likelihood of accepting information that disagrees with those opinions as being either true or meaningful. Also, being open to new ideas and having a curiosity about new things increases the likelihood of "seeing" novel solutions.

Although the openness to experience trait is most closely associated with innovation, by itself it doesn't explain the differences in innovation we see across individuals, even those with similar amounts of knowledge and motivators. Two of the other traits have been shown to increase our understanding of the differences in innovation levels across individuals—conscientiousness and extraversion.[25]

Innovation is hard work. To innovate, one has to develop sufficient knowledge and must go through a difficult problem-solving process. High levels of conscientiousness are associated with a greater level of commitment to a task and a greater willingness to put a large amount of work toward achieving the task. Conscientiousness reflects the degree of ambition and commitment of the individual. A high level of conscientiousness, by itself, does not explain differences in innovation: there are numerous highly conscientious individuals who do not create innovations. However, an individual low on conscientiousness is much less likely to be innovative because he or she is less willing to put in the required effort.

The relationship between extraversion and innovation is

much less clear. As we have seen, innovation is clearly a social process, and the power of learning from others is critical to the innovation process. This does not require the individual to be an extravert, however, as individuals can clearly increase their knowledge base, and therefore their innovation potential, by reading publications of new research and theories. Innovation potential, then, does not come simply from the knowledge gained from direct social interactions, which is the hallmark of extraversion. The importance of extraversion relates more to the desire to communicate the innovation. If someone creates an innovation but never discusses it with others, then the innovation will never be recognized.

Earlier we mentioned Gregor Mendel's groundbreaking work in genetics and how this innovation was not recognized for years. Mendel lived the secluded life of a monk and had relatively little contact with other scientists of his time. Mendel also didn't promote his innovation beyond the publication of his results. The role of conscientiousness and extraversion in innovation is poignantly summed up by one of the central figures in the development of the Big Five framework: "Conscientious individuals may complete their creative projects more often; extraverts may exhibit them more readily."[26]

While it is likely that a high degree of openness to experience has always been an important personality trait of innovators, there is evidence that being conscientious and extraverted is becoming increasingly important to innovation. Two insightful trends have emerged that indicate these two traits are becoming more important. First, the importance of conscientiousness is likely to be increasing as both the average age of newly minted doctorates and the average length of time required to complete a doctorate has increased over the past century.[27] In addition, the average age of a person whose innovation led to a Nobel Prize has also increased throughout this time. This trend has been explained as a consequence of the information explosion. That is, as more and more knowledge is developed on a topic, the amount of knowledge necessary to become an expert in a field continues to increase.[28] This implies that obtaining a doctorate requires a greater degree of conscientiousness today than it did a century ago.

The second trend that has emerged is the increasing number of patents with multiple inventors and the increase in the number of coauthors on peer-reviewed articles.[29] In response to an ever-increasing knowledge base, one approach is to narrow the focus of expertise—to specialize. Despite the increased amount of knowledge required to become an expert in the field, which has translated into longer learning periods, we have also seen an increase in the degree of knowledge specialization over the past century as well. Thus, in order to deal with the rapidly expanding knowledge base, becoming an expert in a subject requires learning more total information than before and requires learning more about a narrowly focused area. Both strategies are required to offset the knowledge explosion. The result is that it is becomingly increasingly necessary to collaborate with others to have the necessary total knowledge available to innovate in many fields. Collaboration requires individuals who are capable of seeking out the right partners and who are capable of working amicably and productively with those partners—extraversion.

The importance of collaboration highlights the significance of understanding the dynamics that lead to innovative and productive teams. The Big Five personality model is very instructive in helping to develop the most innovative and productive teams. Teams require a critical balance of the important personality traits to be successful. That is, the familiar horseshoe pattern emerges when we look at the team's personality, group dynamics, and innovativeness.

Of the three traits related to individual innovation—openness to experience, conscientiousness, and extraversion—it is conscientiousness that has the simplest relationship to group innovation. All else being equal, a group with a greater average level of conscientiousness is more innovative (as well as more productive in general). Thus, groups that are more diligent and focused—conscientious—are, not surprisingly, more innovative and more productive.[30]

The relationship between the average level of extraversion in a team and its degree of innovativeness is also fairly simple to understand, especially for teams working in physical proximity to each other (as opposed to virtual teams). Extraversion and teamwork show the familiar horseshoe pattern—if the average amount of extraversion is low (i.e., the group is comprised of introverts), then innovation is low. Innovation increases as the average amount of extraversion increases, but only up to a point. Once the average level of extraversion gets too high, team innovativeness declines. Quite simply, too much extraversion tends to lead to an excessive amount of non-task-related social interaction.[31]

The relationship between openness to experience and group innovation is the most complex. In highly functioning groups, innovation increases as more individuals with a high degree of openness to experience join the group. In fact, the amount of innovation seems to increase exponentially—similar to the effect that increasing knowledge has to innovation. However, for poorly functioning groups, innovation actually decreases exponentially with the addition of individuals with a high degree of openness to experience! In poorly functioning groups, the volume of initial innovative ideas and solutions is high, but the group fails to build additional combinations that mark truly innovative groups. The net result is that the total innovative volume reduces to the sum of each of the individual innovations, failing to capitalize on the synergistic potential.[32]

The importance of group dynamics to overall innovation cannot be overstated, but they are difficult to measure. There are a couple of features of highly functioning groups, however, that are clear: democratization of ideas—groups that are dominated by a single voice, either due to title, experience, or stature, are not much more innovative than the dominant individual; and openness to disagreement—the successful group has to accept disagreements,[33] up to a point (beyond which disagreements can become destructive). Still, one of the most famous failures of group performance is what is known as *groupthink*, where the group tends toward a single solution without sufficient consideration of alternatives.

The academic community employs these two features— democratization of ideas and openness to disagreement—very successfully. In particular, the double-blind peer-review process does an exceptionally good job of ensuring that every idea gets heard. In addition, it is generally part of the academic culture to accept disagreement on most topics. Even academia fails, nonetheless, when certain theories become so indoctrinated in the community that any challenge to the established view is considered as necessarily flawed.

Taking an even broader view, a historical look at innovation has found that certain periods and places have had much greater innovation than others, while some periods have been nearly devoid of innovation. The best explanation for these large-scale differences relates to the degree of acceptance of diversity of opinion. In dictatorships, for example, the amount of innovation has been shown to be much lower than in more open societies. The same is true of organizations and even classrooms where those that follow a democratic approach to evaluating ideas have much greater innovation than those that follow a dictatorial approach.

The importance of a democracy of ideas is critical to innovation. Next we will explore the democratic revolution and the recent explosion across the world in democracies. This revolution has profound implications for the future of global innovation and progress.

Chapter 5

THE DEMOCRATIC REVOLUTION

If you have ever looked at the map of Asia, and I mean *looked* at it, you would notice that sitting right between China and Russia, two of the world's largest and most powerful countries, is the little-known country of Mongolia. Mongolia has a total population of less than 3 million people, which is dwarfed by both China, which has a population over 1.3 billion, and Russia, which has a population of over 140 million. Despite Mongolia's relative stature in the region, the country stands out as one of the most impressive examples of the modern democratic movement.

Although it sits between fiercely communist China and Russia, which is still strongly controlled by the former Communist Party, Mongolia has followed a path of increasing democratization for the past quarter century. Despite its unique position on the map, Mongolia is just another country of literally dozens of countries that have moved to a democratic form of government over the past generation. During the past twenty years, democratic governments have spread to every habitable continent. We now live in an age where more than one-half of the world's population lives in a democracy. Surprisingly, the democratic revolution, which is based on a fundamental reconceptualization of political authority and human rights, is well over three hundred years old, yet has been growing faster in the past generation than at any other time in history.

While the American Revolution is considered the start of the democratic revolution, the intellectual birthplace of the American Revolution occurred, ironically, in England over one hundred years prior to the Declaration of Independence. The mid-1600s in England was a period of intense intellectual, social, and political upheaval. The scientific revolution overtook England, as well as the rest of Europe, during the first half of the seventeenth century. This period was marked by rapid technological and scientific development, including the invention of the telescope, barometer, and thermometer as well as the first scientific books on magnetism, circulation, and chemistry. But it was the reconceptualization of *how* science is done that proved to be the most important breakthrough.

The new approach to human understanding was crystallized in the beginning of the seventeenth century by Francis Bacon, who has achieved lasting fame, not for being one of the new scientists, but for laying out the framework for a new approach to understanding nature—the scientific method. The scientific method espoused by Bacon called above all for a rigorous application of inductive logic and a strong commitment to data-based knowledge.[1] The new approach was in stark contrast to the traditional Aristotelian approach to science, which valued deductive reasoning and harmony over inductive reasoning and data. For the last 1,500 years, European thought had been dominated by Aristotle's philosophy and religion. In fact, the intellectual pinnacle of the Middle Ages is often considered to be the work by St. Thomas Aquinas to integrate Aristotle's scientific and philosophic works with the Bible.[2] The scientific revolution showed that these deeply ingrained intellectual prejudices were unsupported by data. As a result, the very foundation of the

Aristotelian approach to human understanding was now called into question. Intellectually, the floodgates were now open: man needed to develop new theories as to why the world acted as it did that were not based on preconceived notions.

This new approach was applied in numerous areas, including the source of man's ultimate ability to know anything for certain. The uncertainty surrounding what man *knew* from what man merely *believed* led René Descartes to use the scientific method to develop a radically new approach to understanding human knowledge. Just like any good inductive scientist, Descartes attempted to build his theory from the most basic facts. For Descartes, the most basic, undeniable fact is the famous *"Cogito ergo sum"*—"I think therefore I am."[3] Descartes proceeded to build up a new philosophy of human knowledge from this fundamental fact, and his novel ideas quickly spread across Europe.

Descartes' groundbreaking books—*Discourse on Method*, published in 1637, and *Meditations of First Philosophy*, published in 1641—came during a period of intense political turmoil in England. By 1640, England was at war with both Scotland and Ireland in what was known as the War of Three Kingdoms.[4] Although the war began as a battle over the rights of the king to dictate religion to his subjects (Scotland and Ireland were ruled by England at the time), the limits to the extent of the king's authority in nonreligious matters became an important point of conflict. For the *Meditations of First Philosophy*, Descartes asked seven distinguished intellectuals to provide "objections" to Descartes' ideas. Thomas Hobbes, a well-to-do Englishman who was friends with many of the leading intellectual lights of the time, including Darwin and Kepler, was one of those who provided objections.[5]

With England in political turmoil, Hobbes clearly recognized the need to develop a "scientific" foundation for the government. As a result, Hobbes applied a Descartes-like inductive approach to determine the rights and appropriate structure of government. Hobbes's intent was to use the strict rationalism of the scientific method and the inductivist approach of Descartes to develop a scientific foundation for political power. The result was *The Leviathan*, a highly controversial and influential book outlining the roots of political power, which laid out the intellectual foundation for the democratic revolution.

Just as Descartes developed his theory of knowledge from the most basic form of knowledge, Hobbes developed his theory by imagining an extremely primitive society, perhaps the society that man existed in thousands of years ago, a society without any government. In this governmentless society, man was in what Hobbes famously called a "state of nature."[6] In this state, since there was no authority with power over any person, every person had unlimited rights and no formal obligations. As a result, each person was at liberty to do whatever he wanted. At first blush, many would consider this an ideal state of peace and harmony. While everyone may desire to live a peaceful, content life in this state of nature, Hobbes was rather pessimistic about the consequences, and he famously characterized life in this state of nature as "nasty, brutish, and short."[7]

The cause of Hobbes's pessimism stemmed from the natural needs and desires of man. He opined that in a world of finite resources, more than one person will ultimately want something that can be had by only one person. This leads to conflict, which, Hobbes argued, will necessarily turn into a state of war. In this situation, according to Hobbes, anything goes: "nothing can be unjust."[8] Even for those who would be perfectly content with their lot in life, the state of war exists because these people must constantly be on the defensive against others—it is a war of "every man against every man."[9]

In such a world, Hobbes argued, the only rational thing to do would be to give up certain rights in order to ensure peace. Hobbes argued that people would, either explicitly or implicitly, jointly *contract with each other* and willingly transfer their rights to an agreed-upon authority in return for their personal safety. This is the first use of the "social contract," which is the intellectual foundation on which democracy has been built ever since. This is also in direct contrast to the historical view that a government is given its authority by God, thus emphatically rejecting the divine right of kings.

Ironically, Hobbes actually wrote *The Leviathan* to *justify* dictatorship, particularly the authority of King Charles. The defense of dictatorship rests on the notion that in order for the government to have sufficient power to uphold the law, the government must be above the law. For Hobbes, even a despotic dictator is preferred to the risk of going back to the state of nature, where death is nearly certain. Given the role that Hobbes's theory plays in the democratic revolution and numerous rebellions, it is rather ironic that Hobbes argued that a rebellion is not rational, since it would put a person back into a state of war, which Hobbes considered as basically committing suicide.

In addition to *The Leviathan*, the War of Three Kingdoms resulted in a landmark document outlining specific rights of citizens. The spiraling costs of the war ultimately led King Charles to agree to the Petition of Rights in exchange for additional revenues from Parliament.[10] The Petition of Rights ultimately contained four key elements that show up in most modern-day democracies: (1) the king is required to obtain parliamentary approval for any new tax or loan, (2) subjects cannot be imprisoned without a trial, (3) the use of martial law is banned, and (4) the king cannot force unconsenting citizens to house soldiers.[11] Each of these items has a direct descendent in United States law and most resurfaced as highly charged issues by Americans in the period leading up to the Declaration of Independence.

Despite the agreement on the Petition of Rights, Parliament was unceremoniously dissolved by King Charles (at that time Parliament was called and dissolved only at the behest of the king). Parliament would not be called together for eleven years, representing a period known as the "personal rule" of King Charles. The decision to bring back Parliament to request additional funds, though necessary, would prove fateful as the power struggle between Parliament and the king would lead to civil war.

This war, the English Revolution, ultimately resulted in the beheading of King Charles and the emergence of a political power crisis. In the struggle to determine the source of power and the rights of the government, the country delved deeply into the philosophical and practical foundations of government. In the power vacuum that ensued during the English Revolution and upon the death of the king, Oliver Cromwell became ruler of England in what became known as Cromwell's Protectorate. In many ways, Cromwell was the English version of George Washington—he was an aristocrat who ultimately became leader of the revolutionary army after leading a highly acclaimed military regiment. The similarities did not end there, as Cromwell also refused the title of king and rejected numerous traditional views of the role and authority of the head of the government. In particular, Cromwell rejected the notion of hereditary rule and the idea that his children, merely by virtue of birth, had the right to rule the country.

During this period, political thought in England evolved rapidly, and the role of the rights of the people began to be formalized into England's constitution. The most significant formalization of individuals' rights was embodied in the parliamentary document entitled "An Agreement of the People," arguably the first formal document in the democratic revolution. Notably, the Hobbesian idea of a "social contract" is clearly reflected in this important document. At its core, the agreement represented a statement of the basic principles on which the English government was to be founded, similar in purpose to the US Constitution 150 years hence. In particular, the agreement asserted that individuals had certain basic rights that could not be taken away by the government.[12] The notion that the people have certain rights that could never be infringed upon, even by the representatives of the people themselves, is the other critical political innovation that forms the foundation of the democratic revolution.

As England went through successive transfers of power, the agreement was modified, updated, and replaced by subsequent "core" documents defining the powers and rights of the government. This germination period produced numerous incremental improvements and extensions to the original agreement. Notable in these documents, besides affirming certain fundamental rights, are details regarding the specific mechanics of power, such as the length of time each member of Parliament should sit, controls over decisions about going to war, and limitations of the king. These documents contained numerous innovations in how the government should be run, such as an independent judiciary, that are reflected in the American Constitution today.

Also notable in these documents is the broad powers still assigned to the "king." Oliver Cromwell refused to take the title and even attempted to limit the powers assigned to him, but historical biases toward monarchies, such as the king naming his successor, continued to influence the constitution put forth during this period. Similarly, while the constitution was much more tolerant on religious matters as compared to the reign of Charles and his predecessors, the constitution still required certain religious beliefs and did not make a distinction between church and state. The resistance to change reflects a theme common to all revolutions and one of the biggest challenges to potential revolutions.

This proved to be true in England, as the strong bias toward having a king foreshadowed events in England once the singularly powerful figure of Oliver Cromwell died in 1658. The English constitution and structure of government were not sufficiently stabilized when Cromwell died, and without someone with his leadership abilities to take over, the English revolution faltered. It didn't take long for England to revert to its old ways, as King Charles's son was able to come back from exile and reassert his monarchal authority.[13] While this marked the end of the English Revolution, the intellectual seeds of democracy were sown, and the democratic movement has continued to grow in fits and starts for the last three hundred years.

Under the reign of Charles II, nearly all the constitutional changes were reversed as the newfound rights of the people were lost and the limitations on the power of the king were removed, but the critical foundation had been laid. When political unrest again overtook the country in the late 1680s, leading to what has been termed the Glorious Revolution—so named because the king was overthrown without any bloodshed—the people were able to establish once and for all that they had rights that could never be usurped by any power.

The most important result of the Glorious Revolution was the Declaration of Rights, penned in 1689. The Declaration of

Rights was in many ways a reaffirmation of the rights originally asserted in "An Agreement of the People" and in the Petition of Rights and is a clear precursor to the American Bill of Rights. In particular, the Declaration of Rights asserted that the king could not violate an individual's right to "religion, rights, and liberties."[14] The Declaration of Rights also imposed limitations on the king with respect to Parliament. In particular, the king did not have the right to dissolve Parliament, the king did not have the right to suspend any laws enacted by Parliament, and the king did not have the right to raise a standing army or levy taxes or fees without the consent of Parliament. All these were crucial advances in the balance of power that was so important to the American revolutionaries and to most democratic regimes today.

Similar to the 1630s, the 1680s was a period of political instability in England, generating serious debates on the foundation of political power and the ideal type of government. During this period, John Locke, widely considered as one of England's greatest philosophers and political thinkers, developed his theories on political authority. John Locke was born in 1632, eight years before his father would fight in the civil war that inspired Thomas Hobbes to write *The Leviathan*. Locke attended Oxford and became a professor of philosophy and medicine. His career prospered, and he became a very wealthy and powerful man. Locke also became the personal physician, friend, and ultimately coconspirator for the extremely well-connected Earl of Shaftesbury, who led a group of influential people willing to rebel if Charles II became successor to the throne.

In support of this rebellion, Locke wrote a three-volume political text, of which the second is the most famous, that provided much of the inspiration for the American Revolution a century later. *The Second Treatise of Government* borrows heavily from *The Leviathan* by starting with man in a hypothetical state of nature where men have authority to do as they see fit. Despite starting with Hobbes's conceptual state of nature, Locke comes to a completely different conclusion about the implications of this state. In a fundamental break from Hobbes, the government does *not* receive absolute power to do as it wishes. For Hobbes, the state of nature is so unappealing that any government is preferable to no government. For Locke, the state of nature is not important because it might degenerate into a state of war but because it establishes the rights and freedoms that each person has. Moreover, they would not (reasonably) be willing to give them up to join a society. Therefore, the power of the government is *always* subservient to the will of the people.

For Locke, while the state of nature could turn into a state of war, the real importance of the state of nature is that it establishes the natural equality of every person. This is a "state of perfect freedom to order their actions, dispose of their possessions and persons, as they think fit."[15] Locke's description of the source of these freedoms is strikingly familiar to the inalienable rights laid out in the Declaration of Independence: "man being born . . . with a title to perfect freedom . . . equally to any other man" has a right to control his "life, liberty, and estate."[16] Locke also argued that rebellion was completely acceptable when the government infringed on the critical rights of life, liberty, and estate. Ironically, Locke's writings provided additional support to the intellectual foundation and, more important, the inspiration for some of the leaders of the American Revolution, the first successful democratic revolution in modern times.

Although tensions between the American colonies and England had been building for decades, it was the Stamp Act of 1763 that is often credited as the first step in the inevitable American War of Independence. The Stamp Act was the most hated of a series of taxes imposed on the colonies by England in 1763 in an attempt to have the colonies fund the large cost of defending (and expanding) the English-ruled territory in America. The colonists' resistance to this and other acts derived from the colonies not having any parliamentary representation, which meant they were thus subject to the infamous "taxation without representation." Ironically, the argument against the Stamp Act, that of no taxation without representation was in principle the same argument that Parliament made against King Charles in the Petition of Rights over one hundred years earlier.

Although the king considered the colonies to be in rebellion as early as the summer of 1775,[17] most colonists preferred reconciliation with England. For example, when delegates from each of the thirteen colonies were being selected for the Second Continental Congress (to be held in 1775) and being given instructions as to the wishes of their state, representatives from five of the thirteen colonies had specific instructions to vote *against* independence if the issue came up. In addition, none of the representatives had specific instructions to vote for independence if raised.[18] While the notion that the colonies might decide to declare independence was in the air, it is clear that few members of the Second Continental Congress were planning to push for independence as of late 1775.

The reasons against rebellion could be classified into one of two fears: fear of losing the battle and fear of an even worse government to follow. At that time, England was the strongest country in the world, and the prospects of beating England in a war seemed dim by most colonists. Moreover, England's military strength, particularly its massive navy, provided the colonies with protection against invasion by the other leading nations. England's stable and strong currency provided the colonies with economic stability that would be severely jeopardized if the colonies separated from the mother country. Finally, the prospects of having all the separate colonies being able to maintain a single country seemed a distant prospect at best. Many foresaw each state becoming completely autonomous, a situation that would clearly lead to serious strife.

The rebellion was given an inspirational jolt with the publication of *Common Sense*, the most influential and most widely read political pamphlet of the time.[19] *Common Sense* was published in January 1776, about six months prior to publication of the Declaration of Independence. It was arguably pivotal to the decision of declaring independence, given that the declaration received near unanimous support at the Second Continental Congress.

It is ironic that a recent English expatriate authored *Common Sense*. Thomas Paine moved to America from England only two years prior to writing his pamphlet (Paine also penned the famous line, "These are the times that try men's souls" at the end of 1776 in recognition of the significant deprivation and constant struggle faced by the American troops in the beginning of the Revolutionary War).[20] As a well-educated Englishman, Paine brought with him knowledge of classic English political philosophy, which was dominated at the time by the writings of none other than John Locke (and, to a lesser extent, Thomas Hobbes). *Common Sense* owes a debt to the line of British philosophy that was now well over one hundred years old, which is readily apparent from the first paragraphs. Paine started off *Common Sense* using the exact imagery that

Hobbes and Locke used in describing a state of nature: "In order to gain a clear and just idea of the design and end of government, let us suppose a small number of persons settled in some sequestered part of the earth, unconnected with the rest, . . . [a] state of natural liberty."[21] Unlike his intellectual forebears, however, Paine was less interested in making a philosophical treatise and much more interested in publishing a political position paper. Paine was more than happy to take the conclusions of Locke at face value. In particular, he accepted that the necessary result of such a situation is that the people will create a government with the clear objectives of providing "freedom and security" for its members.[22] In a brilliant stroke, Paine then argued that England failed to provide freedom and security for America.

Regarding freedom, Americans were clearly of the belief that their "freedoms" had already been lost as a result of the Stamp Act and other similar acts of England in which the colonists had no say. Regarding security, Paine points out that being part of England is more likely to bring the colonies into war as it is to protect them: "France and Spain never were, nor perhaps ever will be our enemies as Americans, but as our being the subjects of Great Britain."[23] This simple reversal of common logic was powerful indeed—it was true that Britain was at war or on the verge of war with other European powers for the last several hundred years. The logic was simple and powerful—if England provides neither freedom nor security, then England is not providing the necessary elements of a government, and a new government must be created to provide these fundamental needs.

The philosophical foundations that began with Hobbes, reached their intellectual peak with Locke, and became a rallying cry for the masses through Paine are readily apparent in the Declaration of Independence. Where Locke stated that the obligation of a government is to protect the "lives, liberties, and fortunes of the people,"[24] the declaration famously asserts that all men have "certain unalienable Rights, that among these are Life, Liberty and the pursuit of Happiness."[25] These are the inalienable rights first asserted in "An Agreement of the People" in England over one hundred years prior. Moreover, both the beginning and the end of the declaration holds that a government is formed through mutual, willing consent of the governed—the social contract in action. First, immediately following the list of inalienable rights, the declaration asserts: "to secure these rights, Governments are instituted among Men, *deriving their just powers from the consent of the governed*" (italics mine).[26] To further highlight the importance of the source of governmental authority, the declaration ends with another clear signal that the United States of America was being founded on a social contract: "And for the support of this Declaration, with a firm reliance on the protection of divine Providence, we *mutually pledge to each other our Lives, our Fortunes and our sacred Honor*" (italics mine).[27]

The power of the American Revolution lies in the fundamental reconceptualization of the basis of power for government. This reconceptualization asserts that the ultimate power of the government rests with the people. In the American "experiment," however, which evolved from the political theories that emerged during the political crises in England over the previous 150 years, the extent of this power went well beyond what had been achieved by the political theorists in England. This is made clear through the mechanism by which the president, the king-equivalent in America, is determined: by popular vote of the people. In England, despite the assertion of unassailable rights by the Declaration of Rights, the government remained a hereditary monarchy, which was in stark contrast to the president's being elected every four years by the people in the new republic of America.

This can also be clearly seen in the notion of "no taxation without representation." To the English, representative government meant representation of the classes of people,[28] whereas to the Americans, representative government meant having members come from the region. This explains how both the English and the Americans could see the same "facts" differently—for the English, Americans were represented in Parliament because Parliament spoke for all English subjects; but for the Americans, failure to have any colonists in Parliament meant that Americans were not being represented.

The success of the American Revolution represents a watershed event in the history of the democratic revolution, since America became the first country in modern times to fundamentally reject hereditary monarchy and the divine right of kings and instead place supreme authority of the country with the people. Well, in theory it did. The sad irony is that the political rights and power of most individuals was essentially unchanged in America immediately after winning independence. The real power of the American Revolution was that it didn't end when America became a nation. The true benefits of the reconceptualization of a democratic government are still being worked out in America and throughout the world.

In America, the revolution was just one step in improving the political and legal rights of all individuals and a step that, in fact, provided few immediate gains in power for most Americans. For Americans attempting to craft a government in the wake of actually winning independence, the conflict with a hereditary monarchy was avoided successfully, but embracing a true democracy was a struggle. The most glaring problem was slavery. The famous dictum that each person is equally free to enjoy life, liberty, and the pursuit of happiness was interpreted very differently by different members of the Constitutional Congress.

For many, the notion of having slaves was fundamentally incompatible with the core philosophical foundation of the new government. While some voices at the signing urged for a broader interpretation of who deserves to have their inalienable rights protected, they were in the minority. The subject was so sensitive that, in addition to the debates being held in complete confidence among members of Congress (which was true for every issue the Congress faced), the Congress ultimately compromised by making it illegal to address the issue for twenty years. The resolution to this contentious issue was the Civil War.

The ongoing evolution of the democratic revolution in America can be traced through the ongoing changes to voting rights in America. The ultimate act of power for the people is the right to vote, which helps ensure that the actions of the government represent the people being governed. Despite the high-minded ideals about equality and the appeals to a social contract among equals contained in the Declaration of Independence, the right to vote was a prize available to only a small minority of the population. For example, in the first presidential election of 1788, only white property owners were eligible to vote.

In the United States, the definition of those eligible to vote has expanded over the last two hundred years to include virtually every adult. These extensions required multiple modifications to the original constitution. In 1870, the Fifteenth Amendment to the Constitution was ratified, providing African Americans the right to vote. Since state governments still had the right to impose impediments to voting, such as a "poll tax" or a literacy test, the Fifteenth Amendment had a limited impact on African American voting rates. In 1920, seventy years after the start of the women's suffrage movement, the Nineteenth Amendment to the Constitution guaranteed women the right to vote. Finally, in 1964, the Twenty-fourth Amendment to the Constitution was ratified, eliminating the use of a poll tax. The amendment was further strengthened by the Voting Rights Act of 1965, which banned the use of poll taxes, literacy tests, and any other barrier to voting.

The American Revolution also represented the start of a movement toward democratic regimes throughout much of the world. The inalienable rights of "life, liberty, and the pursuit of happiness" that were elucidated in 1776 and that served as the rallying cry for the colonies in their battle against England also sparked the French Revolution in 1789. In France, Jean-Jacques Rousseau had written a philosophical treatise on the foundation and rights of government power, called the *Social Contract*, which also used the notion of a "state of nature" and an agreement between all people as the foundation for government.[29] In the 1800s, other western European countries followed the lead of America and France (despite the setbacks of the "reign of terror" and the subsequent rise of Napoleon in France) including England and Switzerland. Similar to America, voting rights and other civil rights were initially limited in other democracies and have expanded in the years since. It wasn't until the end of World War I, however, that most European countries adopted some form of a democratic government.

The American Revolution, then, represents just a step in a long evolution in the expansion of political and civil rights both within the United States itself as well as throughout the rest of the world. Democracy, however, is not without competition and has grown relatively slowly throughout most of the past two hundred years. For most of the past two centuries, democracy has been the upstart challenger to the more traditional autocratic regimes (e.g., monarchies, totalitarian regimes, dictatorships, etc.). In fact, after one hundred–plus years of slow growth, primarily via expansion in western Europe, the democratic revolution faced an even newer competitor—socialism. Socialism, which became effectively synonymous with communism, experienced a much more rapid uptake than democracy and quickly rivaled autocracies in the share of the world's population under this new form of government.

The reality is that democracy has only become the dominant type of government within the past twenty-five years. In fact, the democratic revolution has gained greater ground in the last quarter century than it had in the nearly two hundred years previous. This is best illustrated by the results of a look at freedom throughout the world by the nonprofit organization Freedom House. Since 1972 Freedom House has produced an annual report on the state of political and civic freedom in each of nearly two hundred countries. Political freedom is characterized by having a freely elected government, meaningful opposition parties to the ruling party, and a government that is neither controlled by the military nor biased by corruption. In the first report, only 14 percent of all countries were given the highest score (a 1 out of 7) for being politically free. By 2009, this number had doubled to 29 percent. Even if we relax the criteria and look at the percentage of countries given one of the top two ratings (either a 1 or a 2 out of 7) on the political freedom scale, the growth in freedom has been astonishing—increasing from 27 percent in 1972 to 44 percent in 2009.[30] This rapid shift is mostly explained by the increasingly open voting processes in traditional democracies as well as the transition of formerly communist countries to modern democracies. However, this movement has been global in scope, as countries such as South Africa and Mexico have transitioned to democracy.

While voting rights are crucial to a properly functioning democracy, there is an additional core theme of the democratic movement that explains much of the recent rapid movement to democracy. Central to democracy is the maintenance of private property rights. John Locke first highlighted this when he argued that the government couldn't infringe on a man's "life, liberty, or estate." While "estate" became "the pursuit of happiness" in the Declaration of Independence, private property rights have been nearly as critical to the democratic revolution as voting rights. And just as voting rights have evolved throughout the democratic movement, property rights have shown a similar evolution.

As the field of economics advanced in the seventeenth and eighteenth centuries, the concept of property advanced accordingly. While the primary meaning of "property" referred to something physical, such as a plot of land or a horse, economists recognized that property could be intangible. For example, intellectual property was recognized in the form of patents (although patents back then required a physical example to be granted). This tradition carried over into America. For example, property rights in America are primarily protected under what is knows as the "just compensation clause" of the Fifth Amendment to the Constitution, which states "nor shall private property be taken for public use without just compensation."[31]

Although the concept of private property clearly existed prior to the democratic movement, the democratic revolution helped to dramatically increase the protections afforded to private property. For example, while democratic governments still have the right to take an individual's property for the greater good, the rules around compensation for that property have strengthened in support of the owner. More important, the protection of intellectual and "labor" property have evolved considerably in democratic countries. Patent protection has evolved to protect all areas of economic advancement, not just physical products. Labor protection has evolved to protect the value of a person's efforts through laws that ensure safe working environments to laws that protect the wages being provided.

Just as voting rights have vastly expanded throughout the world in the last quarter century, the protection of private property has also seen a dramatic rise in the same time frame. In addition to the annual evaluation of political freedom by Freedom House, the organization also produces a measure of "civil liberties" that includes the degree to which private property is protected. Although Freedom House assesses components other than private property protection in its civil liberties evaluation, the trend in civil liberties is similar to the trend in political liberties. In the 1972 report, only 12 percent of all countries were given the highest score (a 1 out of 7) for their civil freedoms. By 2009, this number had more than doubled to 26 percent. Even if we relax the criteria and look at the percentage of countries given one of the top two ratings (either a 1 or a 2 out of 7) on the political freedom scale, the growth in freedom has been astonishing—increasing from 28 percent in 1972 to 41 percent in 2009.[32] Again, the movement away from socialism, which is based on the concept of public property over private property, is a large driver of this shift.

The collapse of the Communist Bloc has led to a general repudiation of socialist principles and a general acceptance of capitalist principles, of which private property is a cornerstone.

As a result, private property and other capitalist principles are being adopted by countries that have not embraced a democratically elected government. This is most evident in Western Europe, where all of the formerly communist countries have moved toward democratic governments with general elections and a privatization of many formerly government-run industries. While these countries have generally not changed enough to be considered fully democratic under today's terms, they are clearly on the path.

In addition, China has also been shifting from a highly planned economy to an increasingly capitalist economy with rapid economic gains. Over the past thirty years China has been the fastest-growing major economy, with an average annual economic growth rate over 10 percent, and it has become the second largest economy behind the United States. Much of this growth has been fueled by a series of movements toward privatization and capitalism. The first steps began in 1978, when China first started to allow foreigners to invest in special economic zones. This is significant since investors will invest only in countries where they feel their investment will not be confiscated—that is, their private property will be protected. In 1997, China made a major move toward capitalism by making the decision to privatize nearly all the state-owned enterprises. While China has usurped individual rights while supporting economic growth, this movement toward private property rights for businesses is a significant step toward universal property rights. Still, its record on individual rights other than property rights indicates that China has a long way to go toward full democratization.

The movement toward capitalism and greater property rights is significant, as it often leads to greater voting rights. Historical evidence indicates that political power and economic power go hand in hand.[33] In addition, Hernando de Soto, whom Bill Clinton called "the world's greatest living economist,"[34] has argued that the establishment of a system of private property rights will lead to dramatic growth in those countries, primarily the chronically poor, that do not have this system in place.[35] With governments such as China establishing private property rights and allowing economic power to increasingly shift to private companies, there is an increased likelihood that the government will eventually have to make changes in how political power is obtained to accommodate this shift in power.

The expansion of political rights through a continuous movement toward universal voting rights and of property rights through protections for physical, intellectual, and "labor" rights has continued to expand well beyond the original democratic revolutions in England and America in the seventeenth and eighteenth centuries. Due to the failure of a competitor— socialism—and a continued expansion of the meaning of democracy, the growth of the ongoing democratic revolution has accelerated over the past quarter century. The democratic revolution is best understood not by the dramatic upheavals in America or France but rather as a continuous expansion of the ideas about the nature of political power that started in England over three hundred years ago that continue to evolve to this day.

We must recognize, however, that this movement is not preordained to succeed, as there have been many democratic movements that have failed over the years . . . but the picture looks promising.

Chapter 6

FROM INNOVATION TO REVOLUTION

Most innovations fail. This sad fact is well known in the business world, as the vast majority of new products and new companies fail to turn a profit. The same is true for new developments in any human domain: the percentage of innovations that are adopted is very low. To the Darwinian in all of us, the failures are merely the result of survival of the fittest. While this is true in a broad sense, many truly valuable innovations initially fail, only to resurface at a later date.

As noted earlier, the importance of Gregor Mendel's discovery of genetics was completely missed by his contemporaries. Although Mendel's work with the lowly pea ultimately created the field of genetics, he was unable to lead his groundbreaking work through the key steps required to generate a revolution during his lifetime. There are numerous more commonplace examples of innovations that were initially passed over in history. For example, the first seatbelt was patented back in 1885, and by the 1930s prominent physicians were publicly arguing for their use.[1] They did not appear in automobiles until the middle of the 1950s, and even then they were only optional. It wasn't until the late 1980s, when wearing a seatbelt in cars became required by law, that usage became widespread. Even today, for some inexplicable reason, seatbelts are not required for children on a school bus.

143

Perhaps the most famous contemporary business example of an underappreciated innovation is the Windows computer interface. The graphical user interface was invented by the research division of Xerox, then the dominant company for photocopiers, in the 1970s.[2] The corporate leaders failed to recognize the significance of this development and let Steven Jobs, then a young entrepreneur, get the chance to see it before it ever made it to the public.[3] Jobs quickly mimicked and refined the concept and unleashed it to much public fanfare in the Macintosh Apple (although the true winner was Microsoft, who copied the technology when it released Windows to replace its DOS operating system and subsequently became the dominant player in the computer industry).

Developing a novel innovation, then, does not guarantee success. The three main case studies detailed in this book, along with the dozens of other examples evaluated, provide insight into how an innovation leads to a revolution. These examples teach us that in order for innovations to create revolutions, they must pass through three key phases.

RESISTANCE

When a potential adopter first encounters something new, the innovation is evaluated against the current option. This is true even if the innovation is considered to be the first in its class. For innovations that are first in its class, the choice is staying with the status quo (e.g., doing nothing) or adopting the new innovation. In theory, if the innovation is (1) worse than the current option or (2) not worth the cost to switch, then the innovation will not be adopted. This evaluation process is where the vast majority of innovations end—potential adopters evaluate the innovation and decide against adopting it.

The problem with this view is that it assumes a perfectly rational decision maker who has the desire and ability to compare each option completely. This is simply not the way products get adopted. The reality is that people have a natural bias against most innovations. There are powerful psychological forces that create a natural inclination to maintain the status quo in most situations. It is thus important to understand why most innovations die so quickly, even those that seemingly show a clear advantage.

To appreciate the forces at work, we need to understand why the innovator has such a drastically different perception of the new innovation than the potential adopter. The differences in perception arise because each person is looking at the innovation from a completely different frame of reference (there is that Einstein concept again!). As we have seen in the case studies, the final stage of the innovation process is a reconceptualization. This is the source of the challenge. The innovator has gone through the reconceptualization process, but the potential adopter has not.

In order for the potential adopter to understand the idea, then, he or she has to "see" and understand this reconceptualization. That is, the potential adopter must go through a similar process as the innovator. Earlier we illustrated reconceptualization through the analogy of the picture that had two images, the vase or a pair of faces looking at each other, depending on the "reference" point. The ability to switch from seeing the vase to seeing the pair of faces (and vice versa) requires the visual equivalent of a reconceptualization. A similar change in the "reference" point is required not only to create new innovations but also to see the benefit of the new innovation.

Given the need for a reconceptualization, the hallmark of the consideration process is a natural resistance to the new product, service, or idea. From the potential adopter's perspective, the first thing to recognize is that the innovation typically is considered incompatible with the current solution (just as it is impossible to see both the vase and the two faces at the same time). Because the adopter is required to go through the same reconceptualization as that of the innovator, adopting the innovation requires a new way of thinking about the current solution/ product.

Although incompatibility issues raise the bar for a new innovation, the resistance to new innovations typically is heightened when the current solution or product has been successful. Even a current solution or product with many known flaws has already achieved a minimum level of success since it has beaten out numerous alternatives and had some successes. Thus, an innovation has to contend with the bias toward the incumbent, which is based on experience with it.

For example, during the American Revolution, the democratic source of political power was fundamentally incompatible with a hereditary monarchy. Either the people have a say regarding whom they transfer their power to or they do not. In a hereditary monarchy, once the king is established, the people no longer have any say. Although Hobbes effectively argued that people would willingly transfer their power to the king, this would hold only for the first generation. For all subsequent generations, the people would have no say regarding their transfer of political power. (In addition, once the first generation transferred its power, it would no longer have a say either). Importantly, it is not possible to have a hereditary monarchy and a true democracy at the same time; these two forms of government are fundamentally incompatible.

For Einstein's general theory of relativity, the fundamental nature of space was incompatible with the traditional Newtonian view—and one could not hold that both were true. Either space is a fixed container that holds objects—the Newtonian view—or space was defined and shaped by the objects within it—the Einsteinian view. Physicists recognized this incompatibility instantly and were essentially forced to accept one of these as true when developing tests and interpreting results.

Even the World Wide Web, with its flexible approach to the storing of and searching for information, is fundamentally incompatible with the traditional hierarchy-based approach to storing and retrieving information. The World Wide Web and the traditional information storage designs on the Internet in the early 1990s (i.e., the status quo) were in conflict.

When we look at other innovations, many show this same incompatibility between the old and the new. In football, the West Coast Offense was incompatible with the traditional "establish-the-run" philosophy. Keeping with sports, the incompatibility between drafting players based on the advice of traditional scouts, who travel around the country to see high school and college players, or on the advice of the modern-day "scouts," who use advanced statistical analysis of the players without ever seeing them play, is well documented in the popular book *Moneyball*.[4]

In another example, the generation of electricity was originally considered a natural monopoly—where only one firm could successfully and efficiently serve the market—and was historically heavily regulated by the government. Over the last three decades, the industry has been transitioning to a highly competitive market. Although the industry is adopting a process to deal with the transition, the movement to a competitive generation process is incompatible with the traditional closed-loop, full-monopoly system.

The process of deregulation that is occurring in the electricity industry is similar to the deregulation that the telecommunications industry faced in the 1980s (which itself is reminiscent of the trust-busting era in the early nineteenth century). The telecommunications industry was originally conceived of as a natural monopoly with AT&T owning every step in the process. In the 1980s, the industry was restructured to allow for competition in long-distance telephone service while maintaining the monopoly for local service (which has subsequently been changed).

In the automobile industry, it is very difficult to both "go green" and purchase a sports car or SUV. It is not that they are technically incompatible but rather that they reflect incompatible priorities by the adopter. It *seems* contradictory to have a sports car with limited horsepower and torque or a lightweight truck. The original hybrid vehicles were small, lightweight cars that had limited horsepower and torque because the primary objective was to maximize fuel efficiency. This explains why the Toyota Prius was by far the most popular hybrid—it was the only car (by a major manufacturer) that didn't try to solve the incompatible priorities of fuel efficiency and power. While the automobile manufacturers are making hybrid trucks and sports cars now, this represents an expansion of the original idea (which is a critical element of the innovation diffusion process that will be discussed shortly).

The resistance to a new solution or product is also well supported by advances in the evaluation of how humans make decisions under the condition of uncertainty. Because any new product, process, or idea comes with uncertainty, this research has a direct bearing on how people respond to new products.

In the late 1970s, Daniel Kahneman and Amos Tversky, a pair of psychologists, implemented a series of groundbreaking studies that challenged the traditional view by economists of how people make decisions. In the traditional view of the so-called economic man, everyone, when deciding between various alternatives, weighs the costs and benefits of each alternative and chooses the alternative that provides the greatest benefit. In this traditional view, known as expected utility theory, each person, when deciding between alternatives, would multiply the expected benefit of each alternative by the probability of receiving that benefit and choose the alternative with the highest value.[5] Kahneman and Tversky identified numerous instances in which the actual decisions by people violated this traditional view. As a result, they developed a model of how people actually make decisions, called prospect theory,[6] which led to Kahneman receiving the Nobel Prize in economics in 2002 (Tversky also surely would have received the Nobel Prize if he were still alive, but the awards are granted only to those who are living). Let's look at how this works.

One of the principle elements of prospect theory is that people make decisions based on what they stand to gain or lose relative to what they have today. Prospect theory also predicts that people generally are risk averse, at least for small to moderate gains. For example, most people will not be willing to bet one dollar with a 50 percent chance of receiving nothing and a 50 percent chance of receiving two dollars. Under the expected utility theory, people should be equally willing to accept or reject this bet since the expected (i.e., average) return is one. Under prospect theory, people will not choose to take the bet because they are more sensitive to the possibility of losing one dollar then they are to the possibility of gaining two dollars.

Prospect theory also identifies that when a person is expecting to take a loss, he actually tends to be more risk tolerant. That is, he actually will prefer the option that has a higher possible loss (even though it is less likely) in order to increase the chance of anvoiding any loss. For example, if given the choice between losing one dollar for certain or having a 50 percent chance of losing two dollars (which also has a 50 percent chance to lose nothing), most people will take the 50/50 chance. This is contrary to the traditional view of decision making, which predicted that each option would be chosen equally since they both have the same expected return. The reality is that people are so concerned with taking a loss that they will actually choose to risk incurring a bigger loss just to increase their chances of avoiding any loss at all.

This helps explain many anomalies of human behavior, such as the buying and selling of both stocks and real estate, both of which have recently experienced significant boom-bust cycles partially as a result of how individuals deal with losses (along with their overconfidence). The unwillingness to accept a loss explains why individuals will hold onto stocks with an almost irrational fervor. The purchase price sets an emotional floor on the price of a stock, and many individuals will hold onto a stock that has declined for years until they can sell it for more than they bought it. The same is true of real estate purchases, as people are very unwilling to sell a home for less than they bought it for.[7] Homeowners will sell for a loss only in the most extreme economic situations and typically only in the most economically distressed local markets, such as Houston during the oil price crashes of the 1970s, Boston during the savings and loan collapse in the late 1980s, Silicon Valley in the beginning of the 2000s, and Detroit and Las Vegas during the most recent recession.

One of the reasons that most homes do not typically need to sell for a loss is due to inflation. Inflation is basically a chronic condition of the economy where the price of goods and services increases. While the exact rate of inflation is not constant and could be negative, the United States has experienced inflation growth every year for over fifty years. Although high and volatile rates of inflation are damaging to the economy, (which is why one of the primary responsibilities of the Federal Reserve Board is to keep inflation both low and stable),[8] positive inflation actually helps the real estate market function more smoothly since home prices generally go up as a result of the overall increase in price levels (e.g., inflation).

Translating the concepts of prospect theory to the adoption of a new product, process, or idea is straightforward because something new nearly always comes with a greater degree of uncertainty than does what is current. The new product must offer a significant enough potential improvement to overcome the natural tendency to be risk averse. However, the theory also identifies situations that provide greater opportunities for new products than for others. For example, if the expectation is that the current situation will lead to a loss, then a person is more willing to tolerate the risk of adopting a new product. In fact, people will even seek new options that could eliminate the loss altogether even though the uncertainty around these new options could lead to even greater losses.

The implications are clear for new product adoption in the business world: the people in charge of decisions at a company that is declining are much more likely to take a chance on a new product that might help them avoid the loss than will people in charge of decisions at a company that is gaining— even if the new product is expected to help them grow even faster. This helps explain why the American Revolution occurred when it did: the new taxes imposed by the king were leading to economic losses. It has since been documented that political revolutions nearly always occur when economic performance is getting worse.[9] This effect does not always bode well for the democratic revolution, as economically weak democracies are at risk of reverting to authoritarian rule. This also helps explain why the Oakland A's, who were in a deep performance slide, were the first baseball team to incorporate newer statistical methods of evaluating player performance. This helped them become a perennial contender in the late 1990s despite having one of the lowest payrolls in the league.

When evaluating alternatives, both the traditional expected utility theory and the newer prospect theory incorporate the expected benefit of the new product as well as the probability that the new product will actually offer an improvement over the current alternative. As a result, they also both assume that if two people were to agree on both the probability that a new product offers an improvement as well as on the benefit of the potential improvement, then those two people would be equally likely to adopt the new product. Experience with the adoption of new products that have objective statistical evidence of the "superiority" of the new product, however, indicates that adoption patterns vary despite the existence of this objective information comparing the two products.

A theory that has been around for hundreds of years helps to explain why resistance to a new product will vary even in the face of this objective information. Just as there are alternative geometries that are not typically taught in either high school or college geometry classes—which led to Einstein's general theory of relativity—there is an alternative approach to statistical probabilities that is not typically taught in either high school or college statistics classes. In the mid-1700s, a minister named Thomas Bayes proposed a relatively simple theorem about how to calculate probabilities that differs fundamentally from the calculations that are typically taught.

Whereas the traditional calculation of probabilities assumes that the probability of something is an objective fact, the Bayes equation basically argued that probabilities are subjective. In particular, even if two people fully accepted the results of some study regarding the improvement offered by a new product, their ultimate conclusion about the likelihood that the new product would actually offer an improvement could still differ.[10] Why would they differ? Because these two people could have different initial perceptions regarding the likelihood that the new product would actually offer an improvement. Under this theory, the correct probability takes into account both the original assessment as well as this new information. Because they have different original assessments (so-called priors), they also have different final assessments.

An example will help illustrate how this can happen. Let's assume there are two doctors: the first one is just out of medical school while the second one has been practicing for thirty years. Because the first doctor is just out of medical school, she is well armed with the clinical data of the relative ability of the various antibiotics to treat infections. Her perception of each product's performance will be predominantly driven by this clinical data. The second doctor, who has been practicing for so long, has considerable experience prescribing antibiotics to treat infections. His perception of the relative ability of the various antibiotics to treat infections will be based on the clinical studies as well as his actual experience with the product. As a result, if his experience differs from the clinical studies, which it most certainly will at least a little bit, then Bayes's theorem argues that he would have a different view of the relative performance of each product. Thus, if a new study were to come out, these two doctors would incorporate these results and update their perceptions—but they would not come to the same conclusions because of their different prior experiences.

This theory helps explain the different patterns of resistance that are found regarding new products and explains why certain people are much quicker to adopt new products than are others. In particular, this explains why those who are most successful using the old product will be most resistant to the new product—even when presented with the same facts regarding relative performance. The person who has used the old product for a considerable amount of time typically has a higher degree of confidence in its actual performance than someone who has little experience with the old product.

Looking at our case studies, we can clearly see how this applies to them. In the American Revolution, there was a considerable proportion of the American population that was loyal to Great Britain (the Loyalists). The Loyalists were those who tended to be more commercially successful on average than those who chose to rebel.[11] For example, the brilliant Alexander Hamilton was an early advocate of independence, although his mentor Myles Cooper, the dean of King's College (now Columbia University), was one of the most vocal critics of independence.[12] The scientists who adopted Einstein's general theory of relativity tended to be younger scientists who had less experience directly working with Newtonian mechanics. It has been argued that most significant revolutions in science occurred only after those who were trained on and spent their whole careers working with the old system passed.[13]

This pattern is clearly seen in the utilization of the World Wide Web as well as many new technologies. By far, the web was and is dominated by the younger generation in both what is being developed and what is being adopted. For example, the use of e-mail, the most ubiquitous application on the web, was much more quickly adopted by college kids than by their parents. In these applications, it is not necessarily the view that e-mail is unreliable but rather that the expected benefit of using e-mail versus making a phone call is lower for those who have only had the option of making phone calls for the vast majority of their lives. The same age-patern is seen in the adoption of texting and tweeting as means of communications.

CLARIFICATION

The initial resistance to a new product is, in fact, justified since most new products (as well as theories) are not developed and conceived perfectly. The resistance that is often encountered to new ideas actually helps the creator(s) become more precise in honing the exact benefits being offered and the relative value of those benefits compared to current alternatives. In addition, in order for most new products to achieve meaningful adoption, the perceived uncertainty around the performance of the product needs to be reduced.

This explains why, for example, the most successful company in a particular field is not always the company that created the innovation. Famous examples abound. IBM became the dominant force in computers from the 1950s to the early 1990s, even though it did not invent the computer. The original computer was first built for the government during World War II, and the developers, John Mauchly and J. Presper Eckert, created the first computer company immediately after the war. IBM didn't join the party until relatively late, after many of the reliability problems with such components as the vacuum tubes were overcome. Prior to the development of the Prius, Toyota consciously chose a "fast follower" strategy,[14] which enabled it to reduce development costs and to learn from the mistakes of the original innovators.

The commercial airline industry, which also really began after World War II, has a similar history. The British originally launched the Comet for commercial service two years before the development of commercial airplanes even began in America. This delay proved beneficial to the American companies Boeing and Douglas, as these companies were able to learn from the Comet's unexpected metal fatigue and make their products much safer and more reliable.[15]

In the above examples, the innovation typically has high levels of uncertainty at the outset, but this uncertainty rapidly decreases with experience. This reduction in uncertainty is the result of the learning achieved from actual experience with the innovation in real-world situations, situations that even the most disciplined R & D programs cannot match. This effect is known as "learning by doing," and was first characterized by the Nobel Prize–winning economist Kenneth Arrow in 1962.[16]

Arrow's work primarily focused on improvements in efficiency, that is, on reductions in the cost of producing a product, which resulted from increased experience with the actual production process. In traditional terms, production costs would decrease rapidly as a result of learning by doing. Arrow argued that production costs decline due to increased experience, and he developed a mathematical model to predict the rate of decline as a function of the amount of experience.[17]

Since the original developers are first to acquire experience, the original innovator can be in the best position to dominate an industry. However, in industries undergoing rapid change, fast followers have the opportunity to learn from the innovators' mistakes and build improved products and production facilities that take advantage of the current knowledge. Boeing, for example, was able to produce manufacturing facilities with much better tolerance requirements than the original Comet facilities. Thus, the question of whether it is better to be the first to market or a fast follower is really a function of the degree of variability around the initial innovation as well as the degree of flexibility around the production or development process of the new innovation. If the new innovation is, for example, actually an old product for a new application, then the variability around the performance of the product likely will be relatively low, and the company that is first to market will have a stronger position from which to defend against new entrants.

The pharmaceutical industry provides some perfect examples of this process in action. One such example comes from Merck and Company, one of the largest pharmaceutical companies in the world. Merck developed and successfully launched Singulair in the late 1990s to treat asthma, a large and rapidly growing condition. Singulair was subsequently approved for the treatment of allergic rhinitis. It represents the only prescription product approved for the treatment of both asthma and allergic rhinitis, conditions that frequently occur together. Despite going up against some well-established products for the treatment of allergic rhinitis, such as Claritin, Zyrtec, and Allegra, the adoption of Singulair was immediate and rapid as physicians were already comfortable with the product and could easily see how it could treat both conditions.

These examples highlight a general principle of innovation: if the innovation comes with relatively little experience in any other domain, then the developer must expect that there will be reliability problems and must develop a flexible production process. Initially, overinvesting in product automation, for example, is typically not a wise choice for these more fundamentally new products. In capital-intensive industries, however, the initial costs are so high and the recovery time so long, that the initial production decisions will have a considerable impact on the long-term performance of the innovation (and the company). In these situations, the failure rate is very high because the initial innovation almost certainly has unexpected problems and will require modification. The success of the fast follower is much higher for these innovations, where the likelihood of having problems with the innovation is high.

In addition to helping explain why the innovating companies frequently fail to dominate their respective industries, the theory of "learning by doing" explains why most industries experience a similar quality-reduction pattern. In the electric utility industry, the number of days that a customer loses power in one year has dropped precipitously over the last one hundred years, with the vast majority of this drop occurring during the first decades.[17] This is expected—improvements are much greater initially but tend to be smaller as time goes on. This same effect has been documented in numerous industries, such as computer-chip manufacturing, steel manufacturing, and even computer-software development.

The detailed case studies we've examined underscore that considerable uncertainty exists at the onset of even the most significant revolutions. For instance, there was considerable uncertainty about the exact benefits of American independence for many years after the revolution was over. This uncertainty is evidenced by the radically different path the French Revolution took compared to the American Revolution.

Although the general underlying principles were similar for both the American and French Revolutions, the exact specification of the appropriate government to carry out those principles varied considerably. The uncertainties surrounding the appropriate form of government led to considerable distrust among the various revolutionary factions. In France, this distrust became a dominant force and led to infighting and ultimately to the famous "reign of terror" where many revolution-aries were killed in a McCarthy-like search for enemies.

The extreme bloodiness of the French Revolution ultimately caused the revolution to collapse, and the role of king was replaced by the role of the emperor—a king by a different name—and the subsequent reign of Napoleon. This failure had a significant impact on both the speed and the approach to transitioning to a democratic government that had been undertaken by the other European countries. Given the very different turn taken by the French Revolution, it is not at all surprising that the adoption of democracy in Europe was slow: there was much uncertainty surrounding the benefits of democracy (and in many parts of the world that uncertainty still exists).

The same is true of the theory of general relativity, where the verification of the theory did not come until the 1960s. Despite being developed by the most celebrated scientist in the world and being defined by precise equations, there was initially a considerable amount of uncertainty as to the actual performance of the theory in predicting physical phenomena. As discussed previously, the famous tests of the bending of light by the sun performed by Sir Eddington have since been shown to have such a high degree of error that the data actually didn't support Einstein's theory any more than it did the traditional Newtonian theory.[18] However, tests since have corroborated its validity to a very high degree.

ELABORATION

Just as an innovator frequently must struggle to decrease the uncertainty surrounding a new product to gain the confidence of customers, innovations must continue to improve their own product's performance to create a revolution. There are two important dimensions to performance improvement that are frequently overlooked: first, in order to achieve performance improvements, additional innovations are required; and second, the cumulative value of these subsequent innovations is much greater than the value of the original innovation.

The notion that subsequent performance improvements require additional innovations is often overlooked when thinking about innovation, which tends to focus on the spectacular "breakthrough." Perhaps the most famous example of improving performance today is what has become known as Moore's law. It derives from the prediction back in 1965 by the cofounder of Intel, Gordon Moore, that the number of transistors per integrated circuit would double every eighteen months.[19] Moore's prediction remains basically correct; the number of transistors has increased at a pace similar to what Moore predicted forty years earlier. Although Moore no doubt understood the basic concept of diminishing returns and did not actually mean that doubling would go on forever, the real point is that the performance of the integrated circuit has increased rapidly since its introduction.

Nonetheless, in order to increase the number of transistors on a single integrated circuit, engineers and manufacturers needed to develop numerous subsequent innovations, such as more efficient designs, novel materials, and new manufacturing techniques. Similarly, in order to increase the speed of the automobile, engineers and manufacturers needed to develop different engine designs (while the auto industry is dominated by the internal combustion engine, the specific designs of this general class of engines has improved considerably), steering controls, and cooling systems, to name a few.

What has been shown in the semiconductor industry has

been experienced numerous times in other industries: the performance of many innovations increases dramatically after the initial innovation. For example, just as the reliability of electricity generation and transmission has increased dramatically over the last one hundred years, the industry also has experienced a dramatic increase in efficiency. The result was prices that dropped by 90 percent from the beginning of the century until the early 1970s, when electricity prices rose dramatically.[20] Another example is the performance of automobiles. In addition to being prone to breakdowns at a rate dramatically higher than for even the least reliable automobiles today, the top speed of the original automobiles actually was slower than the horse-drawn carriage. Looking at the top speed for the qualifiers of the Indianapolis 500, which started back in 1911, we see that the top qualifying speed continued to increase all the way up to the 1990s.[21]

The other important consequence of these seemingly revolutionary innovations that is likely to be surprising, perhaps even controversial, is that the cumulative value of the subsequent "minor" innovations is much greater than the initial value of the "revolutionary" innovation.[22] For example, despite representing a fundamentally different method of transportation, the initial automobiles had little advantages over the traditional horse and carriage. The initial automobiles were no faster, couldn't travel any farther, and broke down more frequently. In addition, although not intrinsic to the invention of the automobile itself, there was little infrastructure, such as gas stations, to make the automobile useful. Thus, the initial automobiles were basically toys for the extremely wealthy. It was not until improvements in speed, range, and reliability were made, not to mention cost, that the automobile provided advantages over the horse and carriage.

The same is true of the ubiquitous iPod. The first-generation iPod had a maximum storage capacity of 10 gigabytes, supported only audio files, and had a battery life of up to ten hours. Six generations later, the iPod holds up to 120 gigabytes, can play movies and other video files, and has a battery life of up to thirty-six hours. The initial iPod sold exceptionally well due to its sleek design and ease-of-use, but over the years the iPod has become dramatically smaller and more powerful. It has also moved beyond a toy for the teenager to a popular entertainment system for those of all ages.

Another example is the sequencing of the human genome, which was announced with considerable fanfare earlier this century.[23] The innovation, by itself, does nothing to improve the treatment of human ailments. The real value will come as researchers identify specific diseases and conditions associated with specific genes and develop techniques to improve the lifestyle of people with those genes or, perhaps, find ways of "fixing" those genes.

Looking at our in-depth case studies, the initial "versions" were also arguably no better than what they were designed to replace. Their long-term success has been due to their ability to continuously evolve and improve. For the new United States of America, few lives were initially improved once freedom from Britain was achieved. As indicated earlier, one example of this was in voting rights, which initially were available only to basically the same members of society who had those rights before the revolution. The process has been slow, as it took fifty years for landowner requirements to be removed, well over one hundred years for women to achieve voting rights, and nearly two hundred years to achieve voting rights for African Americans.

Even general relativity, which is based on a relatively well-defined set of relationships, has evolved. The most famous is the interpretation of the "cosmological constant." As discussed previously, in developing the theory, Einstein assumed that the universe was static. As a result, he included a "constant" in the equations to support this assumption. When Edwin Hubble discovered that the universe was actually expanding, Einstein realized that his constant was unnecessary. He famously called the constant "the biggest blunder of my life."[24] Similarly, the initial search abilities of the World Wide Web provided results no better than traditional search engines. It was not until the "universal resource language" was completely adopted and improvements were made to the search capability itself that the web enabled greater information retrieval.

When it comes to automobiles, the dramatic increase in speed is only one aspect of improvement. The uses and variations of cars have grown considerably. For example, although the original automobiles were basically the equivalent of large sedans, there are now numerous variations of cars and trucks, ranging from the two-seater sports car, to the minivan, to the eighteen-wheel long-haul carrier. In addition to the numerous vehicle variations, there have been innumerable improvements in the functionality of automobiles. From the mundane, such as headlights and wiper blades, to the cutting edge, such as automatic parallel parking and built-in problem detection, the automobile has gone through numerous incarnations and improvements over the years that have helped sustain the revolution.

As for electricity, although reliability has increased and prices have dropped throughout most of the last century, the real value has come from the innumerable applications that have been developed that use electricity. Although electricity was originally used to provide light, nearly every facet of modern living has been designed to leverage the availability of electricity. This ranges from the cascade of home appliances, tools, and toys through the plethora of office machines to nearly every major industrial application, including even the most extreme energy consumers such as steel making, oil refining, and the like.

Obviously, the computer has come to fill a similar role. From being originally designed as basically a fast calculator, the computer has become a backbone of nearly every industry, office, and household. Although electricity, the computer, and even the automobile are sometimes classified as "general-purpose technologies" (which are defined as technologies that can be applied to numerous applications), we should not overlook the pattern of innovation extension that occurs with every successful innovation.

In examining the extension of these general-purpose technologies, we see similar patterns of innovation and improvements. With something as mundane as the electronic coffeemaker, we can see improvements in terms of the addition of automatic timers, milk frothers, coffee grinders, and various brewing options. In a similar mode, the search engine no longer just finds what is out there but ranks results, searches using natural language commands, and can be modified to select for date, author, and so on.

Even the ubiquitous and lowly paper clip has experienced dramatic improvements and extensions throughout the years. The paper clip is about as basic as it gets in terms of a product, often a two-inch wire bent in such a way as to hold papers. There have actually been dozens upon dozens of inventions related to extensions of the paper clip, such as paper clips with different wire patterns, different materials, not to mention the hundreds of competitive paper-holding devices designed to improve upon this simple object. It became known early on that the paper clip had serious problems holding large volumes of papers and that it was relatively easy it to lose its shape and fail to hold papers securely. While the traditional paper clip has evolved through variations in size and materials to address these limitations, it has also sparked the creation of other binding approaches that have broadened the applicable range of these products.[25]

This effect is seen for nearly every innovation—at first the innovation is not clearly better than the current solution, but improvements and extensions dramatically increase the value of the original innovation. Although many of the extensions will come from the experts who developed the innovation, a significant number of the extensions are identified, and frequently created, by users. Just as improvements are made to innovations from "doing," many innovations are improved by "using."

In the business field, Eric von Hipple, an MIT professor, has spent a large portion of his career documenting the importance of users to the improvements to products. Von Hipple and his colleagues have evaluated the process of innovation adoption and expansion for very specific applications and have identified that approximately one-third of the "problems" with an innovation actually represent extensions of the use of the innovation itself.[26] By responding to these "problems," the innovations continue to expand in their scope, use, and value. In fact, Von Hipple has documented that so-called lead users represent perhaps the greatest source of product innovation. These users place increasing demands on the producer of the innovation, or they actually develop their innovations for the product themselves.[27]

Whereas the concept of learning by doing implies that the quality of an innovation will be improved through experience with building the product, providing the service, or performing the process, the concept of learning by using implies that using the product leads to additional uses, or potential uses, for the product, process, or service—these eventually become new innovations or extensions of the product.

For an innovation to create a revolution, it must be able to successfully pass through the three stages that separate fads from revolutions: resistance, clarification, and elaboration. These three stages act as innovation filters. The vast majority of innovations fail to overcome the natural resistance to new ways of doing things and are cast aside immediately. A select few actually overcome enough of the resistance to achieve some level of success. The product or service that makes it past this point but fails to go through the next stages is best understood as a fad. Since it never evolves, it shines briefly but is overshadowed and overcome by the next innovation. One can think of this as the one-hit wonder in the music industry. In order to go beyond a fad to create a true revolution, the product or service must continue to evolve. The product or service must get more effective, become more reliable, and expand to meet increasingly complex needs. As a result, the successful innovator must recognize that innovation is not an event but rather an ongoing process.

Chapter 7

EMERGENT PROPERTIES OF REVOLUTIONS

In 2008, an intense competition between over one hundred challengers from sixteen countries was organized to determine the best social learning strategy.[1] The competition was unique in one important way: the competitors were not people. Rather, the competitors were computer programs written by specialists from numerous disciplines including management, anthropology, computer science, and sociology.

The rules of the game were simple—in each round the program could choose whether to innovate, learn from others, or work. The objective was also simple—earn the most "money," which was earned only from working. The winning competitor was a fairly complex program written by a pair of professors from Canada. It made statistical "guesses" about the "world" in which it lived, in particular the reliability of the information it received from others.[2] The results of this competition provide extremely valuable insights into the process of social learning, which is at the heart of innovation adoption.

Evaluating the reliability of information received from others is central to the process of innovation adoption. When potential adopters learn about a new innovation, their likelihood to adopt is heavily influenced by the perceived "quality" of the source of information. A recommendation for a health product will typically have a greater influence when given by

C. Everett Koop, the highly regarded former surgeon general of the United States, than a recommendation by an unknown physician. But people rarely make adoption decisions based on a single source. In most cases, people need input from multiple sources. But the input does not need to be a recommendation. The mere fact of seeing others adopt the innovation is an implicit recommendation.

Just as an innovation itself is the result of a social process, the adoption of an innovation is a social phenomenon. And this phenomenon reinforces the one thing everybody knows about social systems—they can be very dynamic and unstable. The notion of "information cascades," where individuals look to what others are doing to decide what they should do, has been used to explain "mob" behavior and underscores how rapidly change can occur.[3] While we are less interested in understanding fads and mob behavior, which occur rapidly but also tend to dissipate rapidly, understanding the factors that influence the speed of product adoption is of paramount importance.

For truly valuable innovations, widespread adoption is more likely to be a matter of *when*, not *if*. But the "when" is critically important to the would-be revolutionary, as the decision to invest the time, energy, and capital is dependent on the likelihood of success *within a certain time period*. The likelihood of an innovation sparking a revolution, and the time it takes for an innovation to propagate through the social system, depends on the specific structure and dynamics of that social system at that time. Let us explore some of the key elements in understanding the pace of innovation adoption.

THE COMPLEXITY CONUNDRUM

While the unknown nature of innovation can lead to excitement about its possibilities, it is much more likely to lead to FUD—fear, uncertainty, and doubt. These three emotions will halt the adoption of an innovation in its tracks. Overcoming these emotional obstacles is critical to adoption, and the easiest way to accomplish this is to show how the innovation is better than the product of the status quo. The problem is that such a direct comparison is surprisingly difficult.

The ideal comparison is the controlled experiment. Perhaps the most advanced version of the controlled experiment is the randomized, double-blind studies performed by clinical drug developers. In these studies, participants are randomly assigned to either the test group or the control group. The test group is given the experimental drug while the control group is given either a comparison drug or a placebo. Importantly, none of the participants know which group he or she is in. In addition, the researchers conducting the study do not know who is in what group. Members of each group are tested for a variety of changes, including any side effects. At the end of the study, the data is evaluated to see whether the groups have any statistically significant differences. If the test group shows a statistically significant difference, then it is assumed these differences are the result of the drug.

This is a very powerful mode of testing, but it is neither feasible in most situations nor as conclusive as it seems. The problem with the randomized study is that it requires a large number of participants and a long time, both typically not possible when evaluating innovations in most areas. Clinical drug developers have a large pool of potential test cases for most of their drugs—people. They also have large budgets, as these tests costs millions of dollars and take years to complete. Most other innovators do not have the luxury of numerous test cases, as the population of possible test subjects is just too small. Worse yet, most innovators face an audience that is unwilling to be the test case. The result is the chicken-and-egg problem—potential test subjects require proof that it will work, preferably in the form of previous test cases (randomly controlled, of course).

When we look at the innovations discussed throughout the book, the ability to compare the innovation to the product or idea of the status quo is just not an option in most cases. This is clearly the case with the democratic revolution, especially in America and western Europe. There is no way to test democracy without trying it, and there were no comparable test cases to study. The only test cases available were approximately two thousand years old and did not end well. The situation was a little better for the general theory of relativity, since the theory made a couple of predictions that could be empirically tested. In neither case, however, could the tests be randomly controlled. The possibility of something else influencing the results could not be ruled out. This is the case with most tests. Even when a test of the innovation versus the product of the status quo is possible, the test can rarely control for all the other possible causes of any difference and rarely has enough test cases to run formal, statistically significant tests.

Sir Eddington's interpretation of the data from the eclipse that was designed to test the general theory of relativity's prediction of the bending of light is a good argument for the double-blind approach. Eddington concluded that the data confirmed Einstein's theory above Newton's, although subsequent reviewers realized that the differences between the two estimates were not statistically significant.[4] Eddington's beliefs seemingly influenced his interpretation of the data. This is why even the researchers in clinical studies are not aware of which patients are being treated with the experimental drug, as it could bias their evaluation or influence their treatment of the study participants. This is also why the scientific community uses a "repeatability" test to evaluate innovations. Since the researcher could influence the study in some unexpected way (or intentionally bias or fabricate the results), nearly every innovation in science that shows promise is tested by a different team of scientists. If the results cannot be reproduced, then the innovation is considered unreliable.

Another common problem when evaluating innovations is a version of the "placebo" effect. In clinical trials, some in the control group consistently experience changes despite being given an innocuous sugar pill. Since the control group wasn't actually given the drug that is being tested, there theoretically should be no changes, but there often are. These changes have become know as the "placebo effect," which has been found in numerous other areas besides clinical trials. The placebo effect is extremely common in business, where an organization adopts an innovation and subsequently sees improved performance. The organization concludes that the innovation caused the improved performance and adopts it more broadly, expecting even greater results. Very often the exciting performance gains disappear. In many cases the cause of the improved performance wasn't due to the innovation itself, but rather due to another factor or the mere fact that a change was made.

The placebo effect underscores a major difficulty when trying to compare an innovation to the status quo: even in randomly controlled, double-blind clinical trials, the results can be exceedingly difficult to evaluate. The drug being tested may show a slight improvement in reducing the symptoms but also may show an unwanted side effect not seen in the current treatment. In addition, the new drug may have been tested in a slightly different population or under slightly different conditions than the current drug, which makes direct comparisons impossible.

The reality is that the decision of whether to choose an innovation over the product of the status quo is rarely made comparing them head-to-head. This makes most innovation-adoption decisions complex, as the decision maker must evaluate numerous variables, many of which are not directly comparable. For innovators looking for converts, complexity is bad. This is because complexity increases the burden on the decision maker, as he or she needs to evaluate each option and weigh the costs versus the benefits. Economists call this a *switching cost*, and they have repeatedly found that the higher the complexity, the higher the switching cost; and as switching costs increase, the likelihood of switching or adopting the innovation decreases.[5]

A complex decision also increases the fear of the unknown. Even though the incumbent may be deficient in certain areas, the decision may often come down to the proverbial "devil you know." When products/services or even theories cannot be directly compared, there is a natural (and justified) concern that the new option might have unrecognized problems. Every innovation comes with a higher degree of ambiguity than the current option, but when faced with a complex decision between a "known" option and a new option, the *perception* of ambiguity increases for the new option. And researches have repeatedly found that as ambiguity increases, the decision maker will increasingly prefer the "known" option.[6]

The problem with complex decisions is that they run

counter to the typical way that people make (or prefer to make) decisions. When making a decision among multiple options, people try to simplify the decision. One of the most common approaches is to identify the single most important attribute and choose the product that performs best on that attribute.[7] This strategy frequently fails, either because there is often no single attribute that is clearly most important or because the differences among the next most important attributes are so large that the mental "trade-off" among multiple attributes must be made. However, when our simplification strategy fails, we are likely to delay making a decision—which again favors the incumbent.

The good news is that these findings provide clear implications for innovators looking to get adopters as well as clear implications for incumbents looking to hold off new competitors. For innovators, the new option must be as simple as possible. In particular, they should identify the most important attribute and, if possible, highlight the innovation's superiority on that attribute. In addition, innovators must do whatever they can to reduce switching costs. In order to get adopters, the innovator must do whatever he or she can to make it easy to switch.

Once the innovation succeeds, it then becomes the incumbent. When a potential new innovation emerges, the adopter will likely be resistant to switching, which he or she will sometimes show to be more complex. And often it is, since it may require customization, which makes comparisons to competitors much more difficult. For incumbents, increased customization increases the "stickiness," and frequently the complexity, of the product, making it that much more difficult for new competitors.

THE REVOLUTIONARY FLU

The rate of adoption of innovations is driven by inertia, decision complexity, and risk aversion . . . most of the time. Researchers in biology, economics, politics, business, and science have all found that there are certain "periods" where change is almost normal and innovations have a much greater chance to thrive. Understanding the characteristics of these periods and when they occur provides some insight into understanding when a revolution will occur and take hold.

In the early 1970s, Niles Eldredge, the curator in the Department of Invertebrates at the American Museum of Natural History, and Stephen Jay Gould, the late professor of zoology at Harvard University, came to the controversial conclusion that one of the cornerstones of Darwin's theory of evolution was incorrect. The theory of evolution argues that changes to species occur gradually over millions of years through the simple processes of random variation (which is represented by the numerous differences between members of a single species) and natural selection.[8] Ever since Darwin proposed his theory, evolutionary biologists recognized that the fossil record was "spotty." That is, the fossils that were found for a species tended to show little variation for vast stretches of time. In some regions, however, the fossil record was considered to be fairly strong with considerable variation showing up in relatively short periods of time. The spotty record was generally considered to be the result of the inconsistency in the fossil preservation process.[9]

But in a move reminiscent of Einstein, Eldridge and Gould were willing to accept that the fossil record represented the actual history of species development. That is, they argued that the failure to find gradual fossil changes was because populations didn't typically evolve gradually. Instead, they contended that populations experienced long periods of relative stability in terms of species change, which are interrupted by short periods of rapid species change. After this brief period of rapid change, the records indicate that another long period of relative stability ensues. The long periods of stability reflect ecosystems in a state of equilibrium, which is interrupted by a short burst of species change and variation. Not surprisingly, they called this "punctuated equilibrium."[10]

Eldridge and Gould also noticed that these periods of rapid change were not limited to a single species but tended to reflect rapid changes in numerous species at the same time. It is as if the whole ecosystem went through a dramatic shift at the same time—which it did. The net result was a dramatically different ecosystem, where different individual species evolved rapidly and where the relative roles of different species changed. This modification to evolutionary theory did not overturn the view of random variation—within any population, numerous random genetic combinations and mutations are occurring constantly. The real change to the theory was in the *process* of natural selection, which was now seen as occurring very rapidly. In a period of equilibrium in the ecosystem, any potentially advantageous genetic combination will be selected for and result in increased survivability, but so will the "traditional" genetic composition. Without *favorable* selection, however, this potentially advantageous genetic combination will not be able to become dominant in a population.[11] Only when the environment changes in such a way that the reproduction rate for the "new" genetic combination is much higher than the reproduction rate for the "traditional" genetic combination will the population show any shifts. These environmental changes tended to happen relatively rapidly.

The same phenomenon is observed in the economy, as long periods of relative economic stability are interrupted by relatively short periods of rapid change.

While it is instinctive to think that recessions represent the periods of rapid change, this isn't altogether correct. It is true that during a recession (as well as the more anomalous depression), there is a rapid change in corporate fitness, which shows up as a spike in layoffs and corporate bankruptcies.[12] Similarly, the sources behind these periods of upheaval tend to start with a shock that disrupts the whole economy. The current subprime mortgage crisis, the dot-com crash in 2001, the late 1980s stock market crash, the spike in interest rates in 1982, and the oil price spikes in the 1970s all represent shocks that rippled throughout the economy and led to economic contractions.

During each of these recessions, and in all the other recessions, corporate failures increased. Using the survival-of-the-fittest view, these companies were not fit to survive in the new economic realities. The problem with recessions is that they tend to represent an overall retrenchment across the whole economy more than a dramatic restructuring of the economy.[13] In biology, the periods of rapid change represent changes in the whole ecosystem and changes in the species that dominate the ecosystems (or parts of the ecosystem). In most (not necessarily all) economic recessions, however, the companies that dominate the economy prior to the recession are usually the same companies that dominate the economy at the end of the recession.

In addition, recessions are much more frequent than we realize. The National Bureau of Economic Research, a non-profit research organization with over one thousand of the nation's leading economists as research associates, is the organization that "officially" classifies the beginning and the end of recessions. Since the end of World War I, the US economy has undergone a recession approximately once every four years, and the typical recession has lasted a little over one year.[14] We were making progress up until the Great Recession, which "officially" began at the end of 2007 and lasted eighteen months. Excluding the Great Recession, ever since the end of World War II the US economy has had a recession approximately every five years that lasted only ten months.[15] Given the frequency of recessions and the fact that they typically do not lead to a major restructuring of the economy, recessions are more like growing pains in a society that is learning how to manage itself rather than a wholesale change to the commercial landscape.

One simple way to see how the frequent recessions have not dramatically altered the landscape of the economy is to look at the largest companies in the United States over time as reported by *Fortune* in their annual ranking of the five hundred largest US companies. Just simply looking at the top ten companies over subsequent five-year periods, in which there is typically a one-year recession and a four-year expansion, we see very little movement across time. For example, from 2000 to 2005, a total of seven of the companies were in the top ten in both periods, with the other three changing as the result of significant mergers. The story is similar for nearly every other five-year period back to 1955.

A look at the largest companies in the *Fortune* 500 provides a clear view of the larger trends in the economy over the past fifty years, highlighting a high degree of stability *across* industries throughout much of this time. For example, the oil companies and automobile manufacturers, along with good old GE and IBM, have been mainstays in the top ten throughout this fifty-year time period. In fact, a deeper look (beyond just the top ten) at America's companies highlights just how stable the oil, automobile, communications, and entertainment industries have been. It also underscores that there are clearly winners and losers through this time as well. The losers are steel, chemicals, and rubber/tire manufacturing. The winners are financial service, healthcare, and technology.

The movements *within* particular industries highlight how dramatic movements can be for particular companies. A couple of the largest companies today experienced meteoric rises in very short periods of time. Berkshire Hathaway, for example, rose from the sixty-fourth largest company in 2000, to the twelfth largest company in 2005, to the largest company in 2009. The last company to show that kind of movement to get into the top ten was none other than IBM. In 1955, IBM was the sixty-first largest company in the United States. By 1960, IBM had risen to number twenty-seven, and by 1965 it had broken into the top ten.

While companies are always rising and falling, the rapid movement of Berkshire Hathaway over the last decade and IBM in the 1960s are just a couple of examples of major company movements during these time periods. For example, from the mid-1990s to the middle of the first decade of the twenty-first century, Microsoft rose by over two hundred spots! Over that same time period, one of the other more famous technology companies, Intel, the maker of the computer chip, rose by forty spots. Other notable rising companies were the financial services companies, led by AIG and Citigroup (aside from Berkshire Hathaway). In addition to IBM, the 1960s saw other conglomerates make similarly dramatic rises. Both 3M, the innovative commercial-products conglomerate, and Monsanto, the agricultural and biotech conglomerate, rose twenty-seven spots throughout the decade.[16] The fact that these two time periods experienced the most dramatic company movements reflects the two periods of dramatic restructuring to the economy that have occurred since World War II.

Although there have been approximately twenty recessions over the past one hundred years, a closer look at the structure of the economy reveals four periods of dramatic economic restructuring. These periods along with the relatively long periods of equilibrium between the periods are consistent with the concept of "punctuated equilibrium" in biology. The first wave occurred at the turn of the twentieth century, when the power of economies-of-scale in industrial production pushed industries to consolidate. This was the era of the monopoly as well as the era that created of some of the wealthiest individuals in American history, such as J. P. Morgan, John D. Rockefeller, and Andrew Carnegie. The second wave occurred in the 1920s as 20 percent of all manufacturing capabilities were involved in consolidation. The third wave occurred in the 1960s as corporations merged across industries in the major push toward diversification. The fourth wave occurred from the mid-1990s to the middle of the first decade of the twenty-first century, as the rapid integration of the global economy and the rapid pace of technological progress pushed companies to ensure they could remain competitive in such rapidly changing times.[17]

Importantly, each of these periods occurred during times of rapid economic growth, not stagnation. Thus, while recessions do have a cleansing effect by removing the least fit companies, recessions tend to also come with limited access to capital for significant new investments. The excess labor and on-the-fence capital is, in a sense, waiting for the next best opportunity to show itself. When the economy starts to accelerate and the strongest industries and companies emerge, labor and capital will rush in with the goal of capitalizing on the next great boom. Thus, while shocks that start in one area of the economy clearly can become contagious and cause shocks to other areas of the economy, it is the spread of new growth opportunities that has shown to be a more powerful force in reshaping the economy than recessions. It is the "growth flu" that is much more powerful and infectious than the "recession flu," and it is these periods that show greater universal opportunity for innovations.

We see a similar effect in the main case studies we've covered. One of the primary causes of the economic restructuring in the 1990s and 2000s is the miniaturization of computing power along with the globalization of information via the World Wide Web. The development of the microprocessor has led to a complete overhaul of nearly every area of the economy, as new companies and new products have emerged to better satisfy our wants and needs. The advances in computing power along with the development of the World Wide Web have clearly led to a dramatic change in how we communicate and access information, which has affected every aspect of our economy. While the last two decades can be considered as a continuation of the Industrial Revolution that has been ongoing for hundreds of years, it is better viewed as one of a handful of periods within this broader movement during which we have experienced particularly dynamic change.

Similarly, and perhaps not coincidentally, the last two decades have seen the contagious spread of democracy and its frequent partner, capitalism. This can be attributed to the collapse of communism, which is best illustrated by the unforgettable images of the fall of the Berlin Wall. While the majority of the countries that have adopted both democracy and capitalism, albeit to varying degrees, are part of the old Eastern

Bloc, the fascinating feature of this movement is that it is truly global—a democratic flu. One of the most fascinating aspects of this flu is the impact it has had on China. Although the communist leaders in China have steadfastly refused to let go of any political power, they have recognized that communism is untenable as an economic doctrine. As a result, China has made a dramatic move toward capitalism over the past twenty years, and the results are truly astonishing. China has rapidly shifted from a closed economy to one of the dominant forces in global trade and is now the second-largest economy in the world after the United States.

While the last two decades have seen the most dramatic shift toward democracy in history, there have been other periods of political "punctuated equilibriums." The American Revolution directly led to the French Revolution as well as a general movement, although not as rapid, throughout western Europe toward democracy. In addition, the end of World War I led to another movement toward democracy. We should take caution. Many of the countries that have recently adopted democracy are at risk of reverting to authoritarian regimes. The risk increases with a weakened economy and, with the global economy struggling to rebound, we have already seen that some of the democratic gains made over the last two decades have been lost.[18]

The possibility of a revolution "reversal" is not limited to politics. As one revolution is reaching its apex, the next revolution is already under way. While we tend to think that every successive revolution leads to an improvement, this is not necessarily the case. Not all revolutions are truly for the better.

THE TIES THAT BIND

As revolutions are a social phenomenon, the adoption rate for an innovation is influenced by the nature of the relevant "society." The frequency and type of interactions among the members of that "society" will have a strong influence on the adoption rate. That is, even if the innovation is clearly superior to the incumbent, the rate of adoption will be affected by the following dynamics of the "society." (By *society* I mean a group that can vary considerably in size.)

Size of the Society

Quite simply, the larger the field, the slower the time from innovation to revolution. At the most basic level, if you develop an innovation and need only to convince your spouse to use it, the time from innovation to "revolution" can be exceptionally quick (we are assuming that the innovation is clearly better *and* that your spouse is rational). Of course, the likelihood of convincing your spouse could depend on a lot of other factors, such as whether you are fighting, whether you can afford to do it at the moment, whether your spouse has the time to invest in the comparison, and so on, but at the end of the day, you need to convince only one person (your spouse). Next, if you develop an innovation for your weekend softball team, it then becomes a little harder since you need to convince a lot more people. Again, even if the innovation is clearly superior, the convincing process takes time, and the more people that need to be convinced, the longer the time to gain adoption.

Member Equality

The size of the field assumes that all potential innovation adopters have equal influence on others. This is clearly not the case, as every society has certain people that carry much more influence than others. In the simple example about convincing your weekend softball team about adopting your innovation, if instead this were a professional softball team, you wouldn't need to convince your teammates. Instead you would need to convince only one person—the manager. Of course, authority and influence are not the same in most societies. Most groups have individuals that wield more-than-average influence even though they don't have the formal authority. It is not uncommon in an organization to have recognized "thought leaders" who do not have formal power. (By *thought leader* I mean a person whose opinion on certain topics is highly influential, regardless of his or her official position in the organization.) In these organizations, it may be more necessary to convince the thought leader, who will in turn convince the rest of the organization.

The ability to identify the thought leaders in a society can be very important to accelerating the pace of a revolution, although how important the thought leader is to the rate of adoption varies by type of innovation. Thought leaders are more influential when the value of the innovation is ambiguous.[19] Similarly, thought leaders are more influential when the risk of adopting the innovation is high. In both situations, the thought leaders are believed to have a better sense of the true value of the innovation. In addition, the complexity of the innovation also increases the importance of thought leaders. For many innovations, the complexity is the cause of the ambiguity. In many very specialized and highly technical fields where the complexity is so high, there may be only a small number of people who have the knowledge to properly evaluate the innovation. This is arguably the case for the initial acceptance of the theories of relativity and quantum physics. The net result is that the vast majority of the population has accepted the theory of relativity without ever evaluating it directly.

The ability to get the respected thought leader to adopt your innovation can be enough to speed up the adoption of your innovation, as the adoption by the thought leader is a clear endorsement for everyone else. This approach of appealing to authority is very effective, when available. Of course, getting to the thought leader and getting her to adopt your innovation are not always easy. More important, while it is natural to think of a thought leader as an individual, thought leaders can also be organizations. A perfect example of the power of using organizational "thought leaders" comes from the start-up company Bloom Energy.

Bloom Energy is a manufacturer of fuel cells that has raised over $400 million in investment capital since its inception in 2001.[20] While hydrogen fuel cells have been around for years and have even become the butt of a joke—"Fuel cells are the power of the future . . . and always will be"—because of the exceptionally slow development of this promising technology, Bloom Energy claims to have broken through some critical barriers to make a highly efficient fuel cell. While other companies have made similar claims, what makes Bloom Energy's claim so much more powerful is the companies that have adopted its product.

First, Bloom Energy is backed by some of the most respected venture capital companies in the world. This provides a level of credibility to the company right out of the gate and can be a powerful influence in getting initial customers. More important, however, is the initial list of customers, which include Google, eBay, and Walmart. As these companies are highly successful and are generally considered to be very innovative, their adoption will increase the likelihood of other companies adopting the product. Thus, the likelihood that other companies will adopt Bloom Energy's fuel cells is much higher because a company like Google has adopted it than it would have been if a "typical" company had adopted it.

Member Interactions

In addition to the size of the society and the relative influence of each member within the society, the frequency that members interact with each other is an important element in the speed of innovation adoption. Much of the interest in social networks focuses on the frequency of interactions to understand the flow of information across a network. One of the areas of particular interest is in the so-called network nodes. These are the people who have an unusually higher number of interactions with others.[21] Since they have more connections, these people tend to have a higher influence on the adoption of an innovation.

While the distribution of social networks and the influence of the hubs can vary considerably from one society to the next, most social networks begin to follow what is known as the "power law" pattern.[22] In this pattern, the vast majority of nodes have relatively few connections while a few nodes have a large number of connections. What is extremely interesting about this pattern is that the distribution of links across a network is similar to the distribution of innovations across inventors described earlier. That is, in both the innovation process and the adoption process, a few individuals have a particularly large influence on the outcome.

The phenomenon has become known as the "Small World Problem," and was first described in 1967 by Stanley Milgram, a sociology professor at the City University of New York. Milgram arbitrarily selected a few hundred people in Nebraska and asked them to attempt to get a booklet to a single person in Massachusetts. He asked the participants to mail the booklet to a personal acquaintance "who is more likely than you to know the target person. You may send the booklet on to a friend, relative, or acquaintance, but it must be someone you know personally."[23]

The most famous insight to come out of the study is that, on average, it took only six people to get from the person in Nebraska to the target in Massachusetts. While the average of the study is six intermediaries, the distribution is fairly close to normal and varies from zero to eleven.[24] But it is the average number of intermediaries that has become "stuck" in the public consciousness. This is the source of the popular idea that we are "separated" from anyone else, even the president of the United States, by only six people. It is also the inspiration behind the trivia game developed in the 1990s "Six Degrees of Kevin Bacon," in which people attempt to link an actor to Kevin Bacon through films they both appeared in, in as few links as possible. (The game, of course, was a play on the title of the play *Six Degrees of Separation* by John Guare.)

While less famous than the six degrees of separation, another important element emerged from that study. It was found that certain individuals appeared numerous times in the chain. Specifically, 48 percent of the total of sixty-four booklets that reached the target came from one of three people. The author recognized the significance of this component as he indicated that while the conclusion of the approximately six intermediaries was similar to that found in other research, "the study has uncovered several phenomena . . . in particular, the convergence of communication chains through common individuals."[25]

The importance of those who are at the center of a social network has filtered into the way marketers attempt to gain adoption for their products. For those promoting a new product, potential customers are traditionally designated as early, middle, and late adopters, based on the rapidity with which they adopt the new product. The general consensus is that the experience of the early adopters is critical to the ultimate success of the product due to their influence on the adoption or nonadoption of those who are typically slower to adopt. The goal of many marketing programs is to target significant marketing efforts at those individuals who represent "hubs" in the social networks. That is, even if they are not typically early adopters and even if the cost to "acquire" them is well in excess of the expected profits from those individuals, the notion is that getting them to be early adopters will rapidly increase the overall adoption of the product.

One of the areas that tends to get overlooked in the analysis of social networks is the *type* of interaction occurring between the members of the network. The rapid rise of the World Wide Web and e-mail has led to an increased focus on these means of communication relative to "traditional" means of communication. However, the influence of these interactions is much lower than the traditional face-to-face interaction. Despite the ability of technology to make communication between two people a possibility anywhere and at any time, the importance of personal interactions is still critical to the innovation-adoption process. The annual conference is an explicit recognition of the importance of face-to-face interactions to the transmission of information. Regardless of whether the conference is in academia or industry, a primary goal of every conference is to foster individual interactions among the members of that society.

The importance of personal proximity to revolutions is well understood in the relatively obscure field of regional economics. Regional economics is the study of subnational economies—the economy of regions, such as that of a city—and the study of the dynamic flows across regions. One area that is well documented in this field is the presence of what have been termed "agglomeration economies."[26] Economists noticed long ago that a region tended to develop a particular strength in an industry that persisted for long periods. Examples of these agglomerations abound throughout the country and the world. In the United States, examples of industry agglomerations include the pharmaceutical industry in the Philadelphia–New York City corridor, the automobile industry in Michigan, and the high-tech industry in Silicon Valley. The Silicon Valley example is both instructive and ironic—an industry that has been focusing on enabling people to communicate and work together from anywhere would, presumably, have no reason to have a central "hub." Especially since escalating wages would theoretically drive employers to lower-cost regions.

One of the primary reasons for the continued high-tech agglomeration economy in Silicon Valley, as well as the other numerous agglomeration economies, is that the greater amount of personal interactions among members within the industry leads to a greater degree of "knowledge spillovers," or transference of knowledge. There are the informal and semiformal interactions, such as local networking groups, as well as the more formal interactions when a worker switches from one company in the industry to another. It has been found that companies operating within an agglomeration area tend to have higher rates of innovation, higher rates of innovation adoption, and higher productivity than companies that are in the same industry but that are not within the agglomeration area.

Just as the innovation itself is the result of the actions of a community, the adoption of an innovation is the result of the actions of a community. Communities are exceptionally dynamic, as the numerous interactions among the members, both formal and informal, follow the whims of human nature. But it is the community that must be convinced of the value of an innovation, and understanding the structure of the community is crucial to understanding how long it may take to gain the community's acceptance.

While true revolutions are a matter of when, not if, for the would-be revolutionary, time is critical. Being able to understand and minimize the time to adoption is the central challenge to firms, regardless of size, that are looking to gain adoption. Firms must manage adoption risk—time—just as they manage innovation risk. For the start-up, which typically has only one or two products, the risk is extremely high because the company may run out of cash before it has sufficient adoption. For the large firm, launching multiple products can reduce the risk, but the costs of launching products can be exceptionally high, and a couple failures can be nearly catastrophic.

Chapter 8

PREDICTING INNOVATION ADOPTION

Prediction making is both an art and a science. The challenge with most predictions is, whether or not we realize it, that they are based on the past, and the future has a tendency to be very different than the past. When predicting, we tend to draw on a combination of our own instincts and experiences. We use this combination to make predictions every day. Most of these predictions are automatic, and we do not realize that they represent predictions at all. For example, when dribbling a basketball, we predict where the ball will bounce after each dribble. If you have ever watched a child attempt to dribble for the first time, you will realize how much experience this actually takes. The good news is that the bounce of the basketball follows certain rules of physics that can be learned by experience (no physics class needed!).

We also make predictions about other people, such as whether they might cut us off while driving or whether they might get mad at us if we reject an offer for dinner. These predictions are much more difficult because they involve predicting human behavior. While many would argue that human behavior is also controlled by physical laws, it is clear that our behavior is so complex that our confidence in our predictions about the actions and feelings of others is much lower than our confidence in the actions and reactions of inanimate things.

192 THE EVOLUTION OF REVOLUTIONS

The ability to predict human behavior is what is necessary in predicting innovation adoption. Moreover, we are not predicting how an individual will react to a controlled stimulus, which we might get fairly good at with experience. Instead when we make a prediction about innovation adoption, we are predicting how groups of individuals will act, react, and interact. The complexity of the prediction problem becomes exponentially more complicated when we are trying to predict how a group will act. This is the crux of the challenge in predicting the adoption of a new product—how to predict group behavior.

Worse yet, we need to predict group behavior to something new. Therefore, we do not have any prior experience with how they will react to this innovation. True, we frequently have experience in seeing how individuals and groups have responded to prior innovations, which provides some information upon which we can base our prediction. We could, for instance, predict adoption for a new innovation to be equal to the average adoption of the innovations we have experience with. We could get more precise and choose a subset of the innovations that we have experience with and use the average of this smaller group. That is, we could choose a set of "analogues" that seem similar to the new innovation and base our prediction of how people will adopt the newest innovation on how they adopted these analogue innovations.

The challenge with this approach, however, is that we are making numerous assumptions about how similar the newest innovation is to the historical innovations. There are numerous possible sources of differentiation, including differences in the relative advantages of the innovation relative to the incumbent, in the connectedness of the market, and in the consequences of switching. The magnitude of these differences can be significant, which would make using the simple analogue approach highly risky.

Instead of relying on the assumptions in the analogue model, we could try to develop a mathematical representation of the innovation-adoption process. In the business world, there is considerable literature on forecasting, and numerous very sophisticated techniques have been developed for this purpose. While forecasting adoption in any area has significance, a good forecast can be critical. In business, the ability to accurately predict the adoption of a new product is crucial to the financial performance of the company, enabling the company to efficiently allocate its finite resources.

If the adoption of the product is predicted to be lower than it actually is, the company is likely to underinvest in the development and/or the marketing of the product. If development or production costs are fairly high, it could lead the company to decide to either cancel or not undertake the development of the product altogether. If the adoption of the product is predicted to be higher than actual, then the company could over-invest in the development or marketing of the product. The result will be a low (or even negative) return on investment. Depending on the magnitude of the investment relative to the company, it could be financially devastating. In addition, since any company has finite resources, the decision to develop or market a product typically results in the decision to not pursue other opportunities. In economics this is known as the "opportunity cost." These lost opportunities can have a significant impact on the long-term health of the company as competitors with better forecasting abilities may decide to pursue the better-but-forgone opportunity.

In the business world, the forecasting of new product adoption went through a revolution starting in the late 1960s, based on the development of a new approach to forecasting, which has become known as the Bass model.[1] The Bass model is a mathematical representation of the product-adoption process, which is well known to generally follow an S-shaped curve. This S-shaped curve is depicted in nearly every economics and business textbook when discussing the product life cycle. In this model, the S shape reflects the numbers of adopters of the new product relative to the total potential adopters.

Consistent with our findings that the initial innovation must go through considerable improvements to create a true revolution, the original Bass model itself has been refined and enhanced considerably over the years. The original model was built to predict the number of adopters of new "durable" consumer products.[2] A durable product is just a product that lasts a long time, like a washing machine or a car. Since durables last so long, the original model dealt only with predicting whether or not the new product would be purchased. This model did eventually address how to predict products that are purchased frequently, since merely predicting whether or not the product is purchased has relatively little impact on the overall revenues of the product. When a new type of chewing gum comes out, for example, predicting when someone would try the product would not provide much insight into whether that person would buy the gum a second time. Another limitation of the original model was that it constrained the exact shape of the S-curve even though experience clearly indicated that product life cycles did not always match. In particular, the curve was forced to be symmetric around the peak adoption rate, and the peak adoption rate itself was constrained.[3] Over the last forty years, others have developed modifications to the Bass model to address these (and other) issues, and this general class of forecasting models continues to be the workhorse approach to predicting new product adoption.

In many ways, however, the conceptual underpinnings of the Bass model are as important as the mathematical foundation. Underlying the Bass model is a framework about how the adoption process works. That is, in this model, new-product adoption is defined by the two critical components—the first reflects the impact of mass communication, such as television, radio, or Internet advertising; the second reflects the impact of word-of-mouth and the underlying impact of the social network on the adoption of a new product.[4] The word-of-mouth effect, which was identified back in 1969, reflects the core of the popularity of social networks today—talk about a long revolution.

The power of the Bass model, or one of the derivative models, relates to the ability to project the long-term adoption pattern based on the initial adoption rates. The applicability of this class of models is far-reaching. While the model was developed for business, it can be extended to any social application. One of the most obvious applications is to identify the innovation, for example a peer-reviewed paper, that will spark the next revolution in an industry. As discussed earlier, the impact of a paper can be measured by the total number of citations that paper receives. Given the long lead times required to get a peer-reviewed paper published, the rate of growth of citations for a paper is frequently very slow. This is especially the case when the paper is "jumping" from one specialized field to a broader set of applications. The net result is that the ability to evaluate the impact of a paper typically takes a long time, frequently up to twenty years![5] By using a modified Bass model, we could identify those papers that are most likely to create revolutions very early, allowing us to help create and shape the revolution (as well as potentially speed up the revolution).

This is the concept behind the "Top Papers" list reported by the Social Science Research Network (SSRN). The SSRN, which is run as a nonprofit organization, is devoted to the "rapid worldwide dissemination of social science research."[6] This is another example of how the World Wide Web is being used to improve our ability to access information. The SSRN covers nearly all social science disciplines and allows authors to disseminate their research into a central website that can be searched by using author, subject, keyword, and abstract. Papers can by downloaded from the site automatically, and most, but not all, are free. Many of these papers are working papers of articles that eventually make it into a peer-reviewed journal. The first benefit of the SSRN is speed—availability of the article on the SSRN can precede its publication in a peer-reviewed journal by a few months to a couple years. This clearly has the capability to accelerate the innovation process.

One of the challenges to using the SSRN is that it allows papers that have not been peer reviewed to be uploaded to the site. Thus, there is no formal quality check to any of the papers. While this can lead to a mass of low-quality publications, there are some approaches built into the system that allow a user to screen for quality. The first and simplest approach is that a user can use the author as a way to screen for quality. That is, a user can choose to download papers only from the "leading" researchers or, perhaps, only from the top schools in the field. Of course, the next revolution is likely to come from a relative unknown, so this feature is not perfect. Perhaps to help get around this exact problem, the SSRN has built the "Top Downloads" feature, which reports the most frequently downloaded papers over the last month and of all time for each discipline.

If we assume that downloads are a leading indicator of citations and use a modified Bass model to evaluate the trend in downloads, then we could predict both when and how high the peak will be for every paper well in advance of the actual peak. To do this, we could use the Bass model (or one of its derivatives) to look at the rate of downloads over the first year or two to "build" a future adoption "path" for each paper. While this will miss some "slow-growth" papers, it could identify a large number of the future high-impact papers very early. The SSRN is not the only game in town that enables the identification of future high-impact papers. There are various commercial organizations that provide access to citation rates for peer-reviewed journals as well as those for older articles.

All is not ideal, however, since the assumption that a high volume of downloads is a leading indicator of a paper with a high impact has not been verified, and this feedback mechanism can create "download bubbles" for papers. "Download bubbles" reflect papers that become downloaded at a massive volume because most people are curious why others are downloading the paper. (This is the academic equivalent of Paris Hilton, who initially became "famous for being famous." There is some evidence of this lemming behavior, as one of the most popular papers on the site was a legal evaluation of the f-word, which is probably not going to lead to a Nobel Prize or any other revolution but is clearly provocative.[7])

Nonetheless, the Bass model can be extremely valuable in identifying the innovations that have a greater likelihood to lead to future revolutions. But these models have a critical limitation—they require actual data on the uptake of the innovation (e.g., number of downloads or number of citations). While this is a good way to identify those papers that will lead to revolutions, it does not help when trying to evaluate the potential for new commercial products. As indicated earlier, businesses must estimate the potential of the product *before* it is actually launched. A business cannot wait for three to twelve months (or even longer) after a product is on the market to determine whether it will become highly adopted and, potentially, create its own revolution. The business has already made investment decisions that can make or break the success of the product as well as the success of the company.

In order to use these models for products *prior* to launch, one must estimate the word-of-mouth effect and the marketing effects. This is traditionally done by using the analogue approach described above, where these effects will be based on the effects of similar products that have already launched. For instance, when launching a new economy car, one might look at the adoption process of previously launched economy cars. The challenge again becomes finding an appropriate set of analogues. For many innovations, it is not clear what an appropriate analogue is. The decision of which analogues to use is typically based on management's best guess about appropriate analogues, which could be based on the order of entry into the market, perceived degree of "newness," or the perceived complexity of the product. The challenge is that it is not clear whether these are the true reasons for the previous product's uptake. Let's imagine that a company is launching a new hybrid car. It is reasonable to use the adoption patterns of the Toyota Prius and Honda Insight as analogues. Despite their obvious similarity, these may not be appropriate analogues since the market for hybrids may have changed since their launch just a few years ago. There are numerous possible reasons the market might have changed, including a change in gasoline prices or a change in the overall economy. But another likely reason the market has changed is because of the launch of these hybrids. New car buyers may be more or less inclined to buy a hybrid now, since they can learn from the experience of others who have actually owned them.

While the Bass model and its successors can help identify whether a recently launched innovation—whether it is in business, academia, or politics—will likely lead to a revolution, other prediction approaches are necessary to predict the success of an innovation or product *prior* to its introduction to the market. This is where market research comes in. While there are numerous market-research methods, the most common is the traditional survey. Surveys have been used for a long time to help predict the future. Perhaps the most recognized examples are the political surveys used to predict which candidate will win the election or whether a referendum will pass. Surveys are also of great significance in understanding the state of the economy. Economists watch the survey of consumer sentiment and the survey of purchase manager expectations,[8] among others, very closely.

Businesses survey potential customers about both current and future products to ascertain whether they are meeting the needs of the market. There are numerous types of surveys, and the audience being surveyed will vary based on the specific need of the company. For example, sometimes it may be appropriate to survey experts, while at other times it may be appropriate to get a representative sample of all potential customers. In either situation, however, the approach is the same—ask questions designed to understand the potential for the product.

Regardless of the nature of the product, a standard approach to determine the rate of adoption for a new product is to show potential customers a prototype of the product and ask them questions about their interest in it and whether they would purchase this product. While this method may be a mainstay of survey research and seemingly straightforward, the results are not as clear as you might think. It is well known that respondents tend to overestimate their likelihood to purchase the product.[9] In addition, the exact degree of this overestimation can vary considerably. As a result, even when the question is very specific to actual usage, such as "How many times in a month will you purchase brand Y?" or "What percent of your purchases of this type of product or service will be for brand Y?" the researcher must make an estimate of the real value based on the stated value.

This is where the use of analogues comes in again. With a history of stated and actual numbers, a "conversion factor" can be developed. In many industries, historical conversion factors have been developed. A good example of this was depicted on the HBO show *Project Greenlight*, which was a documentary look at a movie-making competition.[10] The competition asked hopeful filmmakers to submit an original screenplay. The winner was awarded a one-million-dollar movie budget. The show documented the whole filmmaking process, from cast selection to rehearsals, to scene selection, to editing. While the show itself was only a moderate success, the second season saw the casting of Shia LaBeouf in one of his first movie roles. In one of the most compelling episodes, an early version of the movie was being shown to a test audience. A market-research firm was on hand to survey the audience members immediately after they viewed the movie. The result of the survey was a "score" based on "stated" enjoyment of the movie that, we were told, had been tracked historically against how movies actually performed. A high score would lead to significant national advertising in support of the film, while a low score could lead to zero advertising spent on the film (the movie received a very low score).

The challenge faced by the market researcher in every industry is to identify the best question or set of questions that provides the most reliable predictor of future innovation adoption. There are numerous possible choices, and many will have some predictive power. The goal is to minimize the prediction error *for each innovation*. That is, the relationship between the survey responses and actual adoption may be good *on average*, but may still provide very bad predictions for each new product.

Much research has been done in this area, and there have been some recent developments that show a lot of potential to help improve the prediction of innovation adoption. In particular, a management consultant at Bain & Company has identified a single question that proved to be a much better predictor of company *growth* than historical approaches. The question has been tested across numerous industries with good, albeit varying, success. While the question itself was tested on companies, not products, and did not directly address the adoption of new products, the question is well suited for evaluating new-product adoption prior to launch.

The single question identified as the best predictor of growth for most companies was "How likely is it that you would recommend [company X] to a friend or colleague?"[11] The most striking element of the question is that it directly addresses one of the components of the Bass model—word of mouth. In light of the theoretical and empirical justification for the Bass model, the question almost seems to be an extension of that research. The concept behind this question is simple: a reliable measure of word of mouth will lead to an improved ability to predict performance. In fact, after some simple recalculating, this question yields what is called a Net Promoter score.[12]

Understanding how this "score" is calculated leads to some additional insight into how to predict innovation adoption. The survey respondent is asked to answer the question using a 0-to-10 scale, where 0 is "not at all likely" to recommend and 10 is "extremely likely" to recommend. Despite having ten possible answers, each respondent is categorized into one of three categories: promoter, neutral, or detractor. If the respondent answers either a 9 or a 10, then he is considered to be a promoter and is given a value of 1. If the respondent answers either a 7 or an 8, then he is considered to be neutral and is given a value of 0. If the respondent answers 6 or lower, then he is considered to be a detractor and is given a value of −1. It may seem strange that a "detractor" would be 6 or lower whereas a "promoter" would be only a 9 or 10, but this merely reflects the fact that respondents have a strong tendency to only use the higher numbers, even if they are dissatisfied. The Net Promoter score is simply the percentage of those who scored a 1 minus the percentage of those who scored a −1. Thus, the maximum Net Promoter score is 100 percent, the minimum is 0 percent, and a score of 80 percent or higher is considered very good.

In addition to the direct measurement of the impact of word of mouth, which reiterates the importance of social networks to innovation adoption, the Net Promoter score also reinforces the significance of specific groups within those surveyed in predicting the ultimate adoption rate. For example, those who are neutral are effectively excluded from the score. From a statistical standpoint, this approach is somewhat unconventional since the exact number of "excluded" respondents is unknown in advance. The standard approach to surveys starts with a desired level of statistical certainty, which indicates how many people need to be surveyed. The average of this group is then calculated, along with the confidence interval around that average. For example, the seemingly ubiquitous opinion polls conducted prior to presidential elections will report that candidate A will receive a certain percent of the vote, say 52 percent, with a standard deviation of plus or minus 3 percent.

That is, using the traditional statistical approach, the pollsters are very highly certain (typically 95 percent certain) that this candidate will truly draw a range between 49 percent and 55 percent of the votes. While the Net Promoter score is seemingly simple, the ability to develop these confidence intervals is much more difficult than for most traditional statistics.

The Net Promoter score is intuitively appealing due to its emphasis on word of mouth, which is a core component of the Bass model, but is not without its challenges. In particular, the relationship between the score and actual adoption rates for new products must first be established. With a history of Net Promoter scores and actual adoption, a "conversion factor" can be developed. And, if products get similar scores but have very different adoption rates, then there may be a need to use analogues once again.

A recent approach developed at MIT offers the possibility to develop reliable innovation-adoption forecasts without any historical calibration, such as the Net Promoter score, or the use of historical analogues, such as most traditional forecasting methods. While still relatively new, the potential for improved predictive ability of this "Bayesian Truth Serum," which leverages the Bayesian statistical approach discussed earlier, is considerable, and this new approach might just cause a revolution in the prediction of new-product adoption.

In this approach, instead of asking one question as for the Net Promoter score, the respondent is asked two questions. While the exact pair of questions can vary, their general structure does not: the first question asks the survey taker to provide his own preference, such as whether he would prefer a new hybrid car in red or blue; the second question asks the survey taker to estimate the preference of others, such as what percentage of others would prefer the new hybrid car in red and what percentage would prefer it in blue.[13] Similar to the Net Promoter score, each respondent is given a score based on how he or she answers these two questions. The calculation of the score, however, is much more complicated. Each respondent's score is based on how accurate he is in predicting what everyone else will prefer as well as whether his own preference is more or less common than predicted. At the heart of the approach is a little-known implication of Bayesian statistics, namely, that your own opinion about what everyone else thinks will be influenced by what you think. This has been found in numerous psychological studies and, in another bout of hyperbole, is "one of the most robust findings in all of psychology."[14]

The logic is straightforward and can be best explained by an example. If you prefer chocolate ice cream over vanilla ice cream, and you are asked to estimate what percent of other people also prefer chocolate ice cream over vanilla ice cream, your estimate of the proportion of the population that is "chocolate choosers" will likely be higher than the percent of the population that actually prefers chocolate. Conversely, the person who prefers vanilla will likely estimate that the proportion of the population that is "vanilla choosers" will likely be higher than the percent of the population that actually prefers vanilla. This is not to say that they both wouldn't agree that vanilla is preferred more overall but that they would likely provide different estimates based on their personal ice cream preferences.

For example, a "chocolate chooser" might estimate that 40 percent of the population prefers chocolate, while a "vanilla chooser" might assume that only 25 percent of the population prefers chocolate. While both believe vanilla is more popular, they have different beliefs as to just how popular vanilla really is. In just one of the numerous tests of this effect, students were asked if they were willing to wear a cardboard sign that said "Repent" and then asked to estimate the percentage of other students that would also be willing to wear the sign. In the study, students willing to wear the sign provided higher estimates of the percentage of other students who would also be willing to wear the signs than those who were not willing to wear the signs themselves.[15]

While this approach is fairly new and will likely be expanded and refined over the next few years, some initial study results are intriguing. In a very interesting study, MIT and Princeton University students were given the name of the largest city in each state (but the students were not told it was the largest) and asked (1) whether it was the capital and (2) the percentage of other students who would indicate that it was the capital. Since for each state they only had two choices—yes, the indicated city is the capital or no, the indicated city is not the capital—a student would be expected to get 25 correct (50 percent) based on random guessing. In terms of percentage correct, neither student population did much better than chance—the typical MIT student got 29.5 correct while the typical Princeton University student got 31 correct.[16]

Since it is very common to look at the average or majority opinion as representing the best choice, the study also looked at the performance of the majority decision. The majority decision did improve performance a little, with the majority opinion rising to 31 out of 50 at MIT and to 36 out of 50 at Princeton University (with 4 ties). While this is interesting and surely supports those who decry the lack of geographical knowledge of even our best and brightest students, the real question is whether the Bayesian Truth Serum could improve the percentage of correct answers. The net result is that out of 100 possible answers (50 states for each school), the majority decision got 69 correct (31 for MIT and 38 for Princeton University—splitting the 4 ties) while the Bayesian Truth Serum predictions got 85 correct.[17] In academic terms, the scores significantly improved, rising from a high D to a solid B average.

In another illuminating study, the Bayesian Truth Serum algorithm was used to predict which team would beat the spread for nine weeks of the 2009–2010 National Football League season. An important distinction between this study and the original is that the correct answer is fundamentally unknowable in the NFL test. That is, while a student may know for a fact that Harrisburg is the capital of Pennsylvania, he cannot know for a fact which team will beat the spread in the upcoming Pittsburgh Steelers–Philadelphia Eagles game. This is also a very difficult test because the spread makes picking the winner much more difficult.

While most people assume that the spread is set to get the volume of bets to be equal on both teams, research by Steven Levitt of *Freakonomics* fame has shown that this is not true. Levitt's research showed that the vast majority of games have very lopsided bets and rare was the game that had a near 50/50 split.[18] Levitt argues that the casinos take advantage of the biases that lead to this lopsided betting behavior to generate profits of 20 to 30 percent. The data from this test of the Bayesian Truth Serum confirmed Levitt's findings, as very few games had a near 50/50 split. The test of the Bayesian Truth Serum also confirmed the ability of this approach to improve prediction performance using popular opinion, as the popular opinion was only right 45 percent of the time in the second half of the 2009–2010 NFL season. By using the Bayesian Truth Serum algorithm, however, performance was dramatically increased, picking the correct team 52 percent of the time.[19]

One of the implications of the Bayesian Truth Serum is that

it explicitly recognizes that treating everyone equally will lead to worse predictions. Both the Net Promoter score and Bayesian Truth Serum are unique in that they leverage a subset of survey responders when attempting to best understand what will happen. The Net Promoter score, for example, focuses on those people who are likely to actively promote or actively detract from the company. Those who are neutral are not included in the score at all, presumably based on the notion that their neutrality indicates their passivity regarding either promoting or detracting and, as a result, their opinions will have relatively little impact on the growth of the company. For the Bayesian Truth Serum, those individuals who are good predictors of others' responses and those who provide responses that are "surprisingly common" provide much greater insight into the future than others.

Both the Net Promoter score and Bayesian Truth Serum represent new approaches to market research that have the possibility of dramatically improving forecasts for new-product adoption. While neither of these will provide perfect predictions, together each can help reduce the uncertainty around this critical activity. In both approaches, responses from a subset of those surveyed provide an unduly large influence on the ability to make accurate predictions. The importance of a subset of respondents is conceptually similar to the importance of hubs in social networks—and this similarity may explain why their performance is so promising.

One caveat, however, is important—the most "informative" individuals are frequently not the currently recognized thought leaders in the field. Those with the greatest insight into how the rest of the society will react to an innovation can come from any part of the society. The power of the Bass model, the Net Promoter score, and the Bayesian Truth Serum is that the "informative few" are *not* chosen beforehand. Rather, the most informative emerge as part of the process.

Chapter 9

THE UNIVERSAL
CONSTANT

"Creative destruction" is the process of how innovations—the ultimate measure of creativity—generate revolutions and the destruction of the status quo. Joseph Schumpeter, one of the most influential economists of the twentieth century, coined this powerful phrase (which is also an oxymoron) over fifty years ago to emphasize the importance of innovations and entrepreneurship to economic growth.[1] In this process, innovations lead to the demise of old products, processes, and beliefs, frequently in a dramatic fashion.

He argued that that economic growth and the resultant increases in standards of living did not result from continued incremental improvements of old products and technologies but through the development of fundamentally new technologies. For example, no matter how many improvements that could have been made to the horse and buggy as a mode of transportation, its value to society would never approach that of the automobile. Innovations in improved harnesses, lower-weight carriages, and so on, would be "sustaining" since they merely extended the performance of the status quo. Schumpeter argued that the improvements made from sustaining innovations are fundamentally less valuable than innovations that completely overthrow the status quo, since the latter create much greater gains in productivity.

Since "Schumpeter's revolution," it is common to distinguish "sustaining" from "disruptive" innovations.[2] Sustaining innovations are those that extend or refine a core process, technology, or idea. Intel, for instance, the longtime leader in computer-chip technology, is racing to stay ahead of the competitors, most notably AMD, by continually increasing the power of its chips. In science, sustaining innovations are those that extend, refine, or reinforce the core beliefs of the scientific discipline. For example, in genetics, the principles of heredity and gene transfer represent the core framework on which genetic research and engineering are built and continue to expand. Even in politics the pattern is similar—"sustaining" political innovation occurs when the political doctrine (e.g., the Constitution) is being extended or refined through amendments, etcetera, whereas "revolutionary" political innovations lead to a complete overthrow of the government.

In industry, a "disruptive" innovation, like the World Wide Web, alters how certain activities are performed and, perhaps more important, dramatically alters the distribution of economic strength within and across industries. The emergence of Google as one of the largest companies in the United States in only a few years is one example of this. In science, a "disruptive" innovation, like Einstein's general theory of relativity, upsets the fundamental assumptions underlying much of the scientific research at the time and, more significant, lessens the importance of much ongoing and recent research. As a result, the scientists that were leaders in the prerelativity world have essentially lost much of their established credibility in that area and must reestablish themselves as experts in relativity. In politics, a "disruptive" innovation, as manifested in a revolution, alters the distribution of power among the members of the society.

The distinction between "sustaining" and "disruptive" innovations seems altogether appropriate, as the vast majority of innovations barely have an impact while only a few innovations lead to revolutions. However, every revolution we've evaluated, including the three main case studies, highlights that this distinction focuses only on the *impacts* of an innovation and fails to capture the whole innovation-to-revolution process. The process from innovation to revolution is universal, but the impacts are not.

We have already delineated the key features of the innovation process—problem identification, germination, and reconceptualization—that underlie all innovations. The process of innovation is similar for both sustaining and disruptive innovations. If there is any distinction in terms of the development of an innovation, it could be characterized only by the degree of "difficulty" of that innovation. We have also discussed previously that an innovation can be explained as the result of a unique combination of facts and ideas. Some innovations may only require combining a relatively small number of facts and ideas together, which is arguably "easier" than those innovations that require combining a large number of facts and ideas (especially from very different fields). That is, some innovations may require a greater number of knowledge combinations and thus could be classified as more difficult or more "surprising" than others. Despite the varying degrees of "difficulty" in developing innovations, there is no clear relationship between the difficulty of the innovation and the subsequent impact of that innovation.

We have also described the key features of the innovation to revolution process—resistance, clarification, and elaboration—

that underlie all revolutions. This process is also similar for the sustaining and disruptive innovations. The distinction between the different revolutions is only a matter of magnitude—some innovations have a greater impact on society as a whole. Interestingly, innovations that are equally impressive and equally difficult to bring to fruition can have very different results, as the vast majority of the most difficult innovations will have little impact while only a few innovations lead to revolutions.

At its core, innovation-to-revolution is about change—how to create change when necessary, how to shape change when it has already started, and how to react to change when it seemingly comes out of nowhere.

A few years ago, *Harvard Business Review* published the results of a survey that asked the two hundred most influential management "gurus" to identify the person who was most influential to them. The list was aptly described as the "gurus' gurus."[3] In total, sixty different people were listed, some surprising and some not so surprising. And the person mentioned more than anyone else was the legendary management theorist Peter Drucker.

Peter Drucker is credited as the founding father of the science of management[4] and devoted his career to understanding, developing, and improving the field. Drucker spent a great deal of time focusing on how we should handle change. In particular, he argued that there are two ways we can approach the uncertain future: we can make the future happen or we can anticipate the future that has already happened.[5] The concept of making the future happen is clear—innovate and create a revolution. The concept of anticipating a future that has already happened is less obvious but equally important. Since there is a lag from the innovation to the revolution, Drucker is referring to the ability to identify the innovation that will create the next revolution. He understood that change is constant and that success requires one to be proactive. My goal throughout this book has not been to just provide an account of change—the innovation-to-revolution process. My goal is to help readers successfully cope in an ever-changing world by making a better future happen and capitalizing on the propitious future that has already happened.

MAKE THE FUTURE HAPPEN

On May 25, 1961, before a joint session of Congress, President John F. Kennedy asked the country to commit to a bold plan:

> I believe that this nation should commit itself to achieving the goal, before this decade is out, of landing a man on the moon and returning him safely to the earth. No single space project in this period will be more impressive to mankind, or more important for the long-range exploration of space; and none will be so difficult or expensive to accomplish. . . . in a very real sense, it will not be one man going to the moon—if we make this judgment affirmatively, it will be an entire nation.[6]

President Kennedy sparked a sense of pride in the country and energized some of the greatest minds to create an achievement that the whole world could look at with awe. Of course, presidents are in a unique position, since they are naturally looked to for inspiration and they command vast resources to commit to their plan. But the most successful leaders at any level are those who see the problem to be solved and inspire others to tackle the problem. This is the most important step in creating the future.

The old adage "those who fail to plan, plan to fail" is true—to an extent. Planning is a necessary and critical component of the innovation-to-revolution process, but only those plans that *both* properly define the problem and inspire others will lead to revolutions. As we've discussed, the link from external motivation to internal motivation is inspiration. Inspiration is the cornerstone of both the search for a solution to a difficult problem and, in many cases, the willingness to adopt an innovation—the revolution. A plan that inspires innovation creates revolutionary companies.

This has considerable implications for organizations looking to increase innovation and create a revolution in the industry. When defining the problem to be tackled, you must tap into the human desire to be a part of something bigger. You must inspire both your employees as well as your customers. This is what truly separates the leaders from the managers and leading companies from the also-rans.

The appropriate plan inspires, but it does not prescribe. There are too many unknowns when both trying to solve a problem and trying to gain converts to lay out a precise plan. Ambiguity is a necessary component of every step in the innovation-to-revolution process. The most successful revolutionaries not only accept ambiguity but also embrace it. If the details are known, then the revolution is over.

The importance of ambiguity is most obvious in the innovation process. Innovation requires creating something new, which is, by definition, ambiguous. For organizations, this ambiguity poses multiple challenges. The most obvious challenge is the risk associated with failure. Failure not only results from an inability to solve the problem; failure can also result due to a competitor who produces a quicker or better solution to it.

Failure is not limited to the innovation process alone, as most innovations fail to create revolutions. Innovations must overcome the natural resistance to change, which increases as the potential for loss increases. Even superior innovations may fail if the environment is not capable of changing. While superior innovations will ultimately prevail, the exact timing of when to undertake risk is not always clear.

Dealing with the possibility of failure, for any cause, requires that one engage in risk management as much as possible. Risk management is best understood by venture capitalists and mutual-fund managers. Venture capitalists recognize that the vast majority of their investments will fail. They also recognize that a few will be wildly successful. As a result, a venture-capital company will look to invest in dozens of companies at once so that the small numbers of big winners will offset the large number of failures. This concept is similar to a mutual fund, where the fund invests in a large number of stocks to spread the risks associated with a single company. Of course, in both cases there are additional challenges to risk, since seemingly unrelated investments can both succeed or fail for the same reasons. Venture capitalists tend to have a special area of focus and will generally invest in numerous companies within the same industry. A contraction in that industry can lead to an unusually high failure rate for all new ventures. Similarly, mutual-fund managers tend to select a specific industry or type of investment in which to put their dollars. Even the funds that are indexed to an extremely broad set of companies, such as the Wilshire 5000, cannot remove the risk associated with aggregate economic performance, such as a recession, which tends to pull down all companies.

Similar to venture capitalists, the largest companies should try to manage risk by investing in numerous innovative projects at once. There are considerable challenges to this approach, however, which puts a limit on the number of projects that can realistically be explored at one time by most companies. First, in many established industries the costs associated with a single project can be so significant as to put a limit on the number of projects that can be funded at once. Second, organizational demands for financially handling everyday business limit the number of new products that can be launched over a given time period. As a result, innovation risk is high for nearly every organization. The risk of not innovating, however, is much higher. The companies that succeed are those that are always looking to create the future through innovation.

In creating the future, the innovator and the would-be revolutionary must strike a delicate balance between acting before the proper preparation/development has been done and delaying too long to ensure that everything is perfect. The reality is that the launch of a new product or theory will certainly be missing some important features, many of which may not even be known at the time of launch. True revolutions do not come out perfectly formed. Rather they start with only partially complete innovations that require considerable additional molding to achieve their true potential. In fact, the total value of the "molding" is typically greater than the value of the innovation itself. A revolutionary innovation is one that provides an opportunity for considerable refinement and enhancements, otherwise it will be just another fad.

The decision to "launch" or go with the idea or product should be based on the ability to compete favorably against the incumbent or the possibility of even another competitor entering first. The old aphorism "Don't let the perfect be the enemy of the good" is particularly relevant to the revolutionary process. If you have developed an innovation that is demonstrably better than the incumbent's solution, then you must bring this to market quickly even if you know that a slight delay will lead to further improvements.

This concept is similar to a time-honored principle in the game of chess, where the player with the advantage must take the offensive.[7] Since the player using the white pieces typically has the advantage because he moves first, it is generally regarded that white must be the aggressor in chess or lose this all-important first move advantage.

While being first to market is by no means a guarantee of success, it is preferable to being second to market, all else being equal. Of course all else is not equal, and the fast followers frequently become the market leaders because they improve upon the mistakes of the original version. This is the result of a failure by the first-to-market firms to continue to rapidly innovate and act. Again, this underscores the importance of action, especially in terms of continuous improvement. The initial launch is only a starting point, even for the first to market, not a finishing point. In order to capitalize on the revolution, one must continue to upgrade the product before the competition does. A revolution is a marathon, not a sprint.

ANTICIPATE THE FUTURE THAT HAS ALREADY HAPPENED

The three main case studies we've discussed clearly show that true revolutions have "long tails." That is, there is a long period where a subset of the population is working on solving a well-defined problem—this is the developmental tail. Similarly, once an innovation is achieved, there is a long period where the product or idea gets introduced to the broader population and gets refined and expanded—this is the adoption tail. The revolutions that are shaping our future are already under way, and our job is to identify them.

There are two ways of identifying ongoing revolutions—identify the innovations that are following this universal pattern from problem solving through innovation adoption. Or identify the people who are creating and shaping the next revolutions. In the innovation-to-revolution process, most innovations start as problem solving within a small community. Members of this community frequently communicate with each other through peer-reviewed papers, industry publications, and conferences. The future revolutions emerge as the community increasingly focuses on certain problems and solutions to those problems. By closely monitoring these communication channels, either formally or informally, we can identify these revolutions-in-the-making.

The formal approach would use the Bass model and its derivatives to look at historical patterns to project a likely future path. To use this tool, however, you need data. In some areas this data is readily available, while in other areas we need to create our own data. We have already discussed the example of using the SSRN, where we could track the number of downloads of a paper over time, as a means of identifying those papers that will cause the next revolution. Similarly, tracking the citation rates for peer-reviewed papers provides another means of identifying those innovations that will have the greatest impact. Even if we cannot formally track downloads and citations, an informal monitoring of which problems and innovations are becoming increasingly discussed within a community will lead us to the source of future revolutions. For those looking to identify revolutions, you must become immersed in the community and look for the patterns in this "chatter."

Monitoring all the chatter, either formally or informally, can take a considerable amount of time. In any one field there are numerous areas being explored, and it is extremely difficult to stay abreast of all the "conversations." Another alternative is to focus on those key individuals who are most likely to create and shape future revolutions. One of the recurring themes in the revolutionary process—from the development of the innovation to the adoption of the innovation and even the ability to predict future adoption—is the importance of a small subset of individuals at each stage of the revolutionary process.

That is, while innovations and revolutions are social phenomena, it is neither the lone genius nor the vox populi that determines the ultimate success. Rather, it is typically a handful of people who determine success at each stage. In many communities, these key individuals can be readily identified. For instance, instead of tracking the download or citation rates for peer-reviewed papers, we could simply focus on the developments by professors at the "leading" schools since future revolutions are more likely to come from the works of these professors than from the professors at other schools. Similarly, in the business community, there are frequently individuals who have become recognized experts in the industry, so monitoring their views can provide a glimpse into the likely future revolutions.

Tracking the innovations and ideas of the recognized thought leaders is an efficient approach to identifying future revolutions, but it is not foolproof. Our case studies clearly indicate that the most preeminent individuals in a field are frequently late (if ever) adopters of the next innovation. That is, the leaders of one revolution are frequently irrelevant, if not antagonistic, to the next revolution.

While there is much we can do to both create the future and anticipate the future that has already happened, the reality is that sometimes the future happens by chance. History is filled with examples of unexpected results that have led to revolutions. The most obvious example is the discovery of penicillin, which started out as the unexpected consequences of an experiment. Instead of dismissing the results as due to an error in the dish preparation, Alexander Fleming decided to explore what was causing the strange result.[8] This exploration into what could have been easily dismissed as an error in the experiment led to a true revolution in healthcare, as penicillin was the first of many antibiotics. Antibiotics have been credited with saving millions of lives and have been one of the primary reasons for the dramatic increase in average life expectancy in the developed world over the past century. Similarly, the Post-it note was created after a failed attempt to create an industrial adhesive.[9] While its implications for society have not been as drastic, the Post-it note has become a cultural phenomenon and has spurned numerous derivative products.

These examples underscore the fact that sometimes success goes to those who are most prepared to capitalize on the unexpected. The challenge in these situations is to identify opportunities for determining when an unexpected result is merely the result of a mistake or whether it really represents a glimpse into a novel way of looking at the problem. This is a particularly challenging issue because there is a lot of noise in any data, and the vast majority of the noise is irrelevant and should be ignored. If one were to investigate every observation that does not perfectly fit with expectations, then one would never progress beyond the exploration stage.

Ironically, as we mentioned earlier, those with the most experience in an area are more likely to "throw out" the novel information when it is truly novel because they have learned from experience that the unexpected information is just noise. This partially explains the U shape that we find in the innovation process: innovation increases as knowledge and experience increase, then innovation tends to decrease as knowledge and experience continue to increase. Of course, the productivity rate is going to be much lower most of the time for the relatively inexperienced since they will waste more time pursuing irrelevant and immaterial leads.

While it is nearly impossible to predict "accidental" revolutions, it is not difficult to identify those periods when the community is particularly ready for a would-be revolution. Opportunities tend to occur in multiple areas at the same time, indicating that there are certain periods that provide greater odds for success than others. These periods tend to start with the recognition that the current approach is failing. In science, this occurs when a crucial experiment fails to support the currently accepted theory. In technology, this occurs when an unexpected failure occurs. The opportunity for great success is afforded to those who can create solutions that help get out of the crisis.

Periods following unexpected crises are particularly opportune for the aspiring revolutionary, as these are the times when people are most receptive to new ideas. Fear of loss is a great barrier to action. Once the loss occurs, this barrier is removed. In many cases it is the relative loss that inspires people to explore new ideas and products. That is, the fear of "falling behind" is a powerful motivator for both innovation as well as adoption. The innovator sees others succeeding and feels he or she is missing out and so jumps into the fray. Similarly, the adopter sees others succeeding after adopting new and bold ideas/technologies/strategies, so he or she also adopts a bold strategy. These periods, which tend to follow the crisis, represent fertile ground for the would-be revolutionary in any field.

The idea that change is constant goes back a long way, appearing in both China and Greece at around 500 BCE. In China, change was identified as a key pillar of the philosophy of Lao Tzu, the founder of Taoism. In Greece, the philosopher Heraclitus developed a theory to explain why the universe must be in a constant state of change.

It is fitting that we find the first writings on the universality of change in Greece, the birthplace of democracy, since revolutions—which are merely dramatic periods of change—can often be democratic. In true revolutions, those few who are the most influential—whether it is in the innovation process, in the adoption process, or in the prediction process—can be anyone in the community. Also, the most influential gain their power not from their personal greatness but rather through the position they come to occupy within the community. As a result, in true revolutions, if one of the influential few were to leave, then another person would emerge with equal importance. The revolution will go on, and those who are leading the revolution merely represent the tip of the iceberg.

That is, revolutions are about people, not products. But revolutions are not about individuals, they are about communities. And the community that is searching for an answer to a problem or working to refine a solution is open to anyone.

Moreover, being a revolutionary is not just for the so-called entrepreneurs and visionaries; rather, it is a must for most of us in our modern economy. Those who understand the revolutionary process, both intellectually and intuitively, are best able to cope in a world that is shrinking by the day and that changes seemingly overnight. As we have explored the revolutionary process, we see that the community goes through a series of stages from problem identification to innovation, to expansion. A revolution in the making thus leaves clear signs. All we need to do is look for them.

NOTES

INTRODUCTION: A Revolutionary Book

1. http://bits.blogs.nytimes.com/2008/09/19/will-this-e-reader-replace-papers/ (accessed April 10, 2010).

2. Michele Gershberg and Maureen Bavdek, "Amazon Could Pay for Kindle Sales Coyness," *Reuters*, December 31, 2009. http://www.reuters.com/article/idUSTRE5BU2CN20091231 (accessed April 10, 2010).

3. Jefferson Graham, "Apple Sells 300,000 iPads in First Day," *USA Today*, April 5, 2010. http://www.usatoday.com/money/industries/technology/2010–04–04-apple-ipad-sales_N.htm (accessed April 10, 2010).

4. Michael S. Hart, "Gutenberg: Project Gutenberg Mission Statement by Michael Hart." http://www.gutenberg.org/wiki/Gutenberg:Project_Gutenberg_Mission_Statement_by_Michael_Hart (accessed April 10, 2010).

5. http://en.wikipedia.org/wiki/Riding_the_Bullet (accessed April 10, 2010).

6. David Ornstein, "Open eBook Forum: 2000 Annual Report / 2001 Strategic Plan & Budget," March 19, 2000. http://www.idpf.org/doc_library/annual%20reports/AnnualReport2000.pdf (accessed April 10, 2010).

7. http://en.wikipedia.org/wiki/Amazon_Kindle (accessed April 10, 2010).

8. Erick Schonfeld, "Is the Kindle Outpacing Early iPod Sales?" February 3, 2009. http://techcrunch.com/2009/02/03/is-the-kindle-outpacing-early-ipod-sales/ (accessed April 10, 2010).

CHAPTER 1: The World Wide Web Phenomenon

1. A&E two-part television series, "Biography of the Millennium," first aired in October 1999.

2. Bernard Grun, *The Timetables of History* (New York: Simon & Schuster, 1991), pp. 199–209.

3. http://en.wikipedia.org/wiki/Johannes_Gutenberg (accessed March 26, 2010).

4. Grun, *Timetables of History*, pp. 211–23.

5. Bertrand Russell, *A History of Western Philosophy* (New York: Simon & Schuster, 1945), pp. 505–22.

6. Roy H. Allan, *A History of the Personal Computer* (London, ON: Allan Publishing, 2001), p. 5.

7. Martin Campbell-Kelly and William Aspray, *Computer: A History of the Information Machine* (Boulder, CO: Westview Press, 2004), p. 72.

8. Paul E. Ceruzzi, *A History of Modern Computing* (Cambridge, MA: MIT Press, 2003), p. 1.

9. Campbell-Kelly and Aspray, *Computer*, p. 73.

10. Vannevar Bush, "As We May Think," *Atlantic Monthly*, July 1945. http://www.theatlantic.com/magazine/archive/1969/12/as-we-may-think/3881/ (accessed March 21, 2010).

11. Joel Shurkin, *Engines of the Mind: The Evolution of the Computer from Mainframes to Microprocessors* (New York: W. W. Norton, 1996), p. 38.

12. Doron Swade, *The Difference Engine: Charles Babbage and the Quest to Build the First Computer* (New York: Viking, 2000), p. 148.

13. Ibid., p. 214.

14. Campbell-Kelly and Aspray, *Computer*, p. 25.

15. Herman H. Goldstine, *The Computer: From Pascal to Von Neumann* (Princeton, NJ: Princeton University Press, 1972), p. 96.

16. Bush, "As We May Think."

17. Ibid.

18. Goldstine, *Computer*, p. 153.

19. Martin Davis, *The Universal Computer: The Road from Leipzig to Turing* (New York: W. W. Norton, 2000), p. 166.

20. Goldstine, *Computer*, p. 191.

21. Bush, "As We May Think."

22. Tim Berners-Lee, "Information Management: A Proposal," 1989. http://www.w3.org/History/1989/proposal.htm (accessed March 25, 2010). The original proposal used the term *mesh* instead of *World Wide Web*.

23. Ibid.

24. Tim Berners-Lee, Response to a Frequently Asked Question. http://www.w3.org/People/Berners-Lee/FAQ.html (accessed March 25, 2010).

25. Janet Abbate, *Inventing the Internet* (Cambridge, MA: MIT Press, 2000), p. 43.

26. J. C. R. Licklider, "Man-Computer Symbiosis," *IRE Transactions on Human Factors in Electronics* HFE-1, pp. 4–11, March 1960. http://groups.csail.mit.edu/medg/people/psz/Licklider.html (accessed March 25, 2010).

27. J. C. R. Licklider, *Libraries of the Future* (Cambridge, MA: MIT Press, 1965), p. xii.

28. Doublas C. Englebart, Letter to Vannevar Bush, May 24, 1962. http://www.stanford.edu/class/history34q/readings/Engelbart/Engelbart_LettertoBush.html (accessed March 25, 2010).

29. Michael A. Hiltzik, *Dealers of Lightning: Xerox PARC and the Dawn of the Computer Age* (New York: HarperBusiness, 1999), p. 65.

30. Abbate, *Inventing the Internet*, p. 186.

31. Ibid., p. 213.

32. Tim Berners-Lee, "The World Wide Web: Past, Present and Future." http://www.w3.org/People/Berners-Lee/1996/ppf.html (accessed March 25, 2010).

33. Berners-Lee, "Information Management."

34. Abbate, *Inventing the Internet*, p. 217.

35. Campbell-Kelly and Aspray, *Computer*, p. 272.

36. Ibid.

37. "Microsoft's Settlement: The End of an Era," TechRepublic.com, June 24, 2003. http://articles.techrepublic.com.com/5100–10878_11–5035167.html (accessed March 25, 2010).

38. Statistics taken from NetMarketShare.com.http://marketshare.hitslink.com/report.aspx?qprid=0 (accessed March 25, 2010).

39. Lawrence Page, Sergey Brin, Rajeev Motwani, and Terry Wino-

grad, *The PageRank Citation Ranking: Bringing Order to the Web* (Stanford InfoLab, 1999). http://ilpubs.stanford.edu:8090/422/ (accessed March 25, 2010).

40. Google website. http://www.google.com/corporate/facts.html (accessed March 25, 2010).

41. Paul Twomey, BBC interview, May 26, 2009. http://www.icann .org/presentations/ (accessed March 25, 2010).

42. Ibid.

43. Tim Berners-Lee, Testimony before the United States House of Representatives Committee on Energy and Commerce Subcommitte on Telecommunications and the Internet, 2006. http://dig.csail .mit.edu/2007/03/01-ushouse-future-of-the-web.html (accessed March 25, 2010).

44. Tim Berners-Lee, Comment on Design Issues. http://www.w3 .org/DesignIssues/LinkedData.html (accessed March 25, 2010).

CHAPTER 2: The Innovation Process

1. Jonathan Baron, *Thinking and Deciding* (Cambridge: Cambridge University Press, 2000), p. 127.

2. Philipp Koellinger, Maria Minniti, and Christian Schade, "I Think I Can, I Think I Can: Overconfidence and Entrepreneurial Behavior," *Journal of Economic Psychology* 28 (2007): 504.

3. W. F. M. De Bondt and R. H. Thaler, "Financial Decision-Making in Markets and Firms: A Behavioral Perspective," in *Handbook in Operations Research and Management Science*, vol. 9, ed. R. Jarrow et al. (Amsterdam: Elsevier, 1995), p. 389.

4. Raymond Nickerson, "Confirmation Bias: A Ubiquitous Phenomenon in Many Guises," *Review of General Psychology* 2 (1998): 175.

5. Allan H. Murphy and Robert L. Winkler, "Can Weather Forecasters Formulate Reliable Probability Forecasts of Precipitation and Temperatures?" *National Weather Digest* 2, no. 2 (1977): 3.

6. Robert J. Sternberg, "A Three-Facet Model of Creativity," in *The Nature of Creativity*, ed. Robert J. Sternberg (Cambridge: Cambridge University Press, 1989), p. 133.

7. John P. Kotter, "What Leaders Really Do," in *Harvard Business Review on Leadership* (Boston, MA: Harvard University Press, 1998), pp. 40–41.

8. Al Gore, *Earth in the Balance: Ecology and the Human Spirit* (New York: HoughtonMifflin, 1992), p. 4.

9. IPCC Third Assessment Report, Technical Summary. http:// www.grida.no/publications/other/ipcc_tar/ (accessed March 28, 2010).

10. IPCC Fourth Assessment Report: Climate Change 2007, Summary for Policy Makers. http://www.ipcc.ch/publications_and_data/ ar4/wg1/en/spm.html (accessed March 28, 2010).

11. US Department of the Treasury, Office of Debt Management, "Presentation to the Treasury Borrowing Advisory Committee (February 2, 2010)," p. 15.

12. Alan Greenspan, *The Age of Turbulence: Adventures in a New World* (New York: Penguin Books, 2008), p. 185.

13. Author's calculations. Office of Management and Budget, "Budget of the United States Government, Fiscal Year 2011 (February 1, 2010)," p. 151.

14. Central Intelligence Agency, *The World Factbook 2009* (Washington, DC: CIA, 2009). https://www.cia.gov/library/publications/ the-world-factbook/rankorder/2102rank.html (accessed March 28, 2010).

15. Jill Wechsler, "Safety Concerns Slow New Drug Review and Approval Processes," *Formulary* (November 1, 2009). http://formulary journal.modernmedicine.com/formulary/Modern+Medicine+Now/Safety -concerns-slow-new-drug-review-and-approval-/ArticleStandard/ Article/detail/640136 (accessed March 28, 2010).

16. Department of Health and Human Services, "Results from the 2007 National Survey on Drug Use and Health: National Findings." http://www.oas.samhsa.gov/NSDUH/2k7nsduh/2k7results.cfm#Ch8 (accessed March 28, 2010).

17. Gretchen Vogel, "New Brain Cells Prompt New Theory of Depression," *Science* 290, no. 5490 (October 2000): 258–59.

18. Matthew J. Bair et al., "Depression and Pain Comorbidity: A Literature Review," *Archives of Internal Medicine* 163 (November 2003): 2441.

19. Michael Lewis, *Moneyball: The Art of Winning an Unfair Game* (New York: W. W. Norton, 2003), p. 59.

20. Charles Mackay, *Extraordinary Popular Delusions and the Madness of Crowds* (New York: Barnes & Noble, 2002), p. xvii.

21. Alan Greenspan, Speech at the Annual Dinner and Francis Boyer Lecture of the American Enterprise Institute for Public Policy Research, Washington, DC (December 5, 1996). http://www.federalreserve .gov/boardDocs/speeches/1996/19961205.htm (accessed March 28, 2010).

22. Robert J. Shiller, *Irrational Exuberance* (New York: Doubleday, 2005), p. 211.

23. Pat Langley and Randolph Jones, "A Computation Model of Scientific Thought" in *The Nature of Creativity*, ed. Robert J. Sternberg (Cambridge: Cambridge University Press, 1989), p. 177.

24. Gordon E. Moore, "Cramming More Components onto Integrated Circuits," *Electronics* 38, no. 8 (April 1965).

25. Karl R. Popper, *Realism and the Aim of Science* (London: Routledge, 1985), p. 134.

26. Mark E. Gaffigan, "Advanced Energy Technologies: Budget Trends and Challenges for DOE's Energy R & D Program," United States Government Accountability Office (March 5, 2008).

27. Pat Langley et al., *Scientific Discovery: Computational Explorations of the Creative Process* (Cambridge, MA: MIT Press, 1992), p. 12.

28. http://www.westcoastoffense.com/history.htm (accessed March 28, 2010).

29. "The Changing Structure of the Electric Power Industry," US Energy Information Administration (1996), p. 1. http://www.eia.doe .gov/cneaf/electricity/chg_stru_update/update 2000.pdf.

CHAPTER 3: The Relativity Revolution

1. Guido Bacciagaluppi and Antony Valentini, *Quantum Theory at the Crossroads: Reconsidering the 1927 Solvay Conference* (Cambridge: Cambridge University Press, 2009), p. 281.

2. Ibid., p. 12.

3. Ibid., p. 10.

4. Neils Bohr, "Discussion with Einstein on Epistemological Problems in Atomic Physics," in *Albert Einstein: Philosopher-Scientist*, ed. P. A. Schlipp (Evanston, IL: Library of Living Philosophers, 1949), pp. 211–24.

5. Werner Heisenberg, *Physics and Philosophy* (Amherst, NY: Prometheus Books, 1999), pp. 42–43.

6. Bacciagaluppi and Valentini, *Quantum Theory at the Crossroads*, p. 270.

7. Albert Einstein, *Letters on Wave Mechanics: Correspondence with H. A. Lorentz, Max Planck, and Erwin Schrodinger* (New York: Philosophical Library, 1986), p. 39.

8. Frank Durham and Robert D. Purrington, *Frame of the Universe: A History of Physical Cosmology* (New York: Columbia University Press, 1983), pp. 156–57.

9. Hans Reichenbach, *The Philosophy of Space and Time* (New York: Dover Publications, 1958), p. 1.

10. Jeremy Gray, *Ideas of Space: Euclidean, Non-Euclidean and Relativistic* (Oxford: Clarendon Press, 1989), p. 34.

11. Marvin Jay Greenberg, *Euclidean and Non-Euclidean Geometries: Development and History* (San Francisco: W. H. Freeman, 1972), p. 127.

12. Gray, *Ideas of Space*, p. 86.

13. Ibid., p. 107.

14. Frank J. Sulloway, *Born to Rebel: Birth Order, Family Dynamics, and Creative Lives* (New York: Vintage Books, 1997), p. 13.

15. Mary B. Hesse, *Forces & Fields: A Study of Acting at a Distance in the History of Physics* (Totowa, NJ: Littlefield, Adams, 1965), p. 150.

16. Heisenberg, *Physics and Philosophy*, p. 3.

17. H. A. Lorentz, "Electromagnetic Phenomena in a System Moving with Any Velocity Less Than That of Light," in *The Principle of Relativity*, ed. A. Sommerfeld (New York: Dover Publications, 1923), p. 11.

18. Albert Einstein, "On the Electrodynamics of Moving Bodies," in Sommerfeld, *Principle of Relativity* (see note 17), p. 38.

19. Albert Einstein, *Relativity: The Special and the General Theory* (New York, NY: Crown Publishers, 1952), p. 44.

20. Albert Einstein, "The Foundation of the General Theory of Relativity," in Sommerfeld, *Principle of Relativity* (see note 17), p. 111.

21. Ibid., pp. 111–12.

22. Michio Kaku, *Hyperspace: A Scientific Odyssey through Parallel Universes, Time Warps, and the 10th Dimension* (New York: Anchor Books, 1994), p. 88.

23. Albert Einstein, "Autobiographical Notes," in Schlipp, *Albert Einstein* (see note 4), p. 67.

24. Henri Poincaré, *Science and Hypothesis* (New York: Dover Publications, 1952), p. 73.

25. Ibid., p. 76.

26. S. Chandrasekhar, "The General Theory of Relativity: Why 'It Is Probably the Most Beautiful of All Existing Theories,'" *Journal of Astrophysics and Astronomy* 5, no. 1 (March 1984): 5.

27. Ibid., p. 3.

28. Ibid.

29. Howard Gardner, *Creating Minds: An Anatomy of Creativity Seen through the Lives of Freud, Einstein, Picasso, Stravinsky, Eliot, Graham, and Gandhi* (New York: Basic Books, 1993), p. 120.

30. Heisenberg, *Physics and Philosophy*, p. 121.

31. http://nobelprize.org/nobel_prizes/physics/laureates/1921/index.html (accessed May 5, 2010).

32. Louis de Broglie, *Matter and Light: The New Physics* (New York: W. W. Norton, 1939), p. 27.

33. Max Born, "Einstein's Statistical Theories," in Schlipp, *Albert Einstein* (see note 4), p. 167.

34. Heisenberg, *Physics and Philosophy*, p. 43.

35. Neils Bohr, "Discussion with Einstein on Epistemological Problems in Atomic Physics," in Schlipp, *Albert Einstein* (see note 4), p. 218.

36. Louisa Gilder, *The Age of Entanglement: When Quantum Physics Was Reborn* (New York: Alfred A. Knopf, 2008), p. 3.

37. J. S. Bell, *Speakable and Unspeakable in Quantum Mechanics* (Cambridge: Cambridge University Press, 2004), p. xxii.

38. Ibid., p. xxvi.

39. Heisenberg, *Physics and Philosophy*, p. 123.

CHAPTER 4: The Nature of Innovation

1. Teresa M. Amabile, "How to Kill Creativity: Keep Doing What You're Doing. Or, If You Want to Spark Innovation, Rethink How You Motivate, Reward, and Assign Work to People," *Harvard Business Review* (September–October 1998): 79.

2. Beth A. Hennessey, "The Social Psychology of Creativity," *Scandinavian Journal of Educational Research* 47, no. 3 (2003): 255.

3. Robert Axelrod, *The Evolution of Cooperation* (New York: Basic Books, 1984), pp. vii–viii.

4. http://space.xprize.org/ansari-x-prize (accessed May 25, 2010).

5. http://www.xprize.org/about (accessed May 25, 2010).

6. McKinsey & Company, "And the Winner Is . . . Capturing the Promise of Philanthropic Prizes," p. 19. http://www.mckinsey.com/clientservice/.../And_the_winner_is.pdf (accessed May 25, 2010).

7. Kevin J. Stiroh, "Playing for Keeps: Pay and Performance in the NBA," *Economic Inquiry* 45, no. 1 (2007): 145.

8. Paul Ekman, "All Emotions Are Basic," in *The Nature of Emotion*, ed. Paul Ekman and Richard J. Davidson (New York: Oxford University Press, 1994), p. 18.

9. Beth A. Hennessay, "Is the Social Psychology of Creativity Really Social? Moving beyond a Focus on the Individual," in *Group Creativity: Innovation through Collaboration*, ed. Paul B. Paulus and Bernard A. Nijstad (New York: Oxford University Press, 2003), p. 188.

10. Viktor E. Frankl, *Man's Search for Meaning* (New York: Pocket Books, 1985), p. 121.

11. John F. Kennedy, "Inaugural Address," in *My Fellow Americans: The Most Important Speeches of America's Presidents, from George Washington to George Bush*, ed. Michael Waldman (Naperville, IL: Sourcebooks, 2003), p. 165.

12. Andy Hertzfeld, *Revolution in the Valley* (Sebastopol, CA: O'Reilly Media, 2005), p. 150.

13. Fernand Gobet and Neil Charnes, "Expertise in Chess," in *Chess in Cambridge Handbook on Expertise and Expert Performance*, ed. K. Anders Ericsson et al. (Cambridge: Cambridge University Press, 2006), p. 523.

14. Neil Charness, "Expertise in Chess: The Balance between

Knowledge and Search," in *Toward a General Theory of Expertise: Prospects and Limits*, ed. K. Anders Ericsson and Jacqui Smith (Cambridge: Cambridge University Press, 1991), p. 43.

15. Larry R. Squire, *Memory and Brain* (New York: Oxford University Press, 1987), p. 131.

16. Donald T. Campbell, "Blind Variation and Selective Retention in Creative Thought as in Other Knowledge Processes," *Psychological Review* 67 (1960): 380.

17. Dean Keith Simonton, *Creativity in Science: Chance, Logic, Genius, and Zeitgeist* (Cambridge: Cambridge University Press, 2004), p. 45.

18. Charness, "Expertise in Chess," p. 50.

19. Simonton, *Creativity in Science*, p. 45.

20. John M. Levine, Choi Hoon-Seok, and Richard L. Moreland, "Newcomer Innovation in Work Teams," in Paulus and Nijstad, *Group Genius* (see note 9), p. 212.

21. Michael A. West, "Innovation Implementation in Work Teams," in Paulus and Nijstad, *Group Genius* (see note 9), p. 254.

22. Simonton, *Creativity in Science*, p. 63.

23. Peter F. Drucker, *Innovation and Entrepreneurship* (New York: HarperBusiness, 1985), p. 139.

24. Bostjan Antoncic, "The Entrepeneur's General Personality Traits and Technological Developments," *World Academy of Science, Engineering and Technology* 53 (2009): 236.

25. Hao Zhao and Scott E. Seibert, "The Big Five Personality Dimensions and Entrepreneurial Status: A Meta-Analytical Review," *Journal of Applied Psychology* 91, no. 2 (2006): 264.

26. Robert R. McCrae, "Creativity, Divergent Thinking, and Openness to Experience," *Journal of Personality and Social Psychology* 52 (1987): 1264.

27. Benjamin F. Jones, "Age of Great Invention" (Cambridge, MA: National Bureau of Economic Research Working Paper Series w11359, 2005), p. 2.

28. Benjamin F. Jones, "The Burden of Knowledge and the 'Death of the Renaissance Man': Is Innovation Getting Harder?" (Cambridge, MA: National Bureau of Economic Research Working Paper Series w11360, 2005), p. 4.

29. Ibid., p. 26.

30. Terry Halfhill et al., "Group Personality Composition and Group Effectiveness: An Integrative Review of Empirical Research," *Small Group Research* 36, no. 1 (2005): 88.

31. Bruce Barry and Greg L. Stewart, "Composition, Process, and Performance in Self-Managed Groups: The Role of Personality," *Journal of Applied Psychology* 82, no. 1 (1997): 62.

32. Simon Taggar, "Group Composition, Creative Synergy, and Group Performance," *Journal of Creative Behavior* 35, no. 4 (2007): 274.

33. Ibid., p. 276.

CHAPTER 5: The Democratic Revolution

1. Bertrand Russell, *A History of Western Philosophy* (New York: Simon & Schuster, 1945), p. 543.

2. Ibid., p. 452.

3. René Descartes, *Meditation on First Philosophy: With Selections from the Objections and Replies*, trans. John Cottingham (Cambridge: Cambridge University Press, 1986), p. 17.

4. Austin Woolrych, *Britain in Revolution* (Oxford: Oxford University Press, 2002), p. 4.

5. Descartes, *Meditation*, p. xxiii.

6. Thomas Hobbes, *Leviathan: Parts One and Two* (Indianapolis, IN: Bobbs-Merrill, 1958), p. 106.

7. Ibid., p. 107.

8. Ibid., p. 108.

9. Ibid., p. 106.

10. Woolrych, *Britain in Revolution*, p. 58.

11. Ibid., pp. 56–57.

12. Ibid., p. 386.

13. Steven C. A. Pincus, *England's Glorious Revolution 1688–1689: A Brief History with Documents* (Boston: Bedford/St. Martin's, 2006), p. 11.

14. Ibid., p. 70.

15. John Locke, *Second Treatise of Government*, ed. C. B. Macpherson (Indianapolis, IN: Hackett, 1980), p. 8.

16. Ibid., p. 46.

17. Bernard Bailyn, *The Ideological Origins of the American Revolution* (Cambridge, MA: Belknap Press of Harvard University, 1992), pp. 152–53.

18. Thomas Paine, *Common Sense*, ed. Isaac Kramnick (New York: Penguin Classics, 1988), p. 8.

19. Craig Nelson, *Thomas Paine: Enlightenment, Revolution, and the Birth of Modern Nations* (New York: Viking, 2006), p. 92.

20. Ibid., p. 108.

21. Paine, *Common Sense*, p. 66.

22. Ibid., p. 68.

23. Ibid., p. 84.

24. Locke, *Second Treatise of Government*, p. 111.

25. http://www.ushistory.org/declaration/document/index.htm (accessed May 24, 2010).

26. Ibid.

27. Ibid.

28. Claude Halstead van Tyne, *The Loyalists in the American Revolution* (Honolulu: University Press of the Pacific, 2004), p. 9.

29. Jean-Jacques Rousseau, *The Social Contract*, trans. Maurice Cranston (New York: Penguin Classics, 1987), pp. 59–61.

30. Author's calculations. http://www.freedomhouse.org/template.cfm?page=439 (accessed May 24, 2010).

31. http://www.archives.gov/exhibits/charters/bill_of_rights_transcript.html (accessed May 24, 2010).

32. Author's calculations. http://www.freedomhouse.org/template.cfm?page=439 (accessed May 24, 2010).

33. F. A. Hayek, *The Road to Serfdom* (Chicago: University of Chicago Press, 1994), p. 16.

34. http://www.unc.edu/news/archives/oct04/fpg_desoto101904.html (accessed May 24, 2010).

35. Hernando de Soto, *The Mystery of Capital: Why Capitalism Triumphs in the West and Fails Everywhere Else* (New York: Basic Books, 2000), pp. 5–8.

CHAPTER 6: From Innovation to Revolution

1. Insurance Institute for Highway Safety, Status Report (1992), vol. 27, no. 3, p. 1.

2. Michael A. Hiltzik, *Dealers of Lightning: Xerox PARC and the Dawn of the Computer Age* (New York: HarperBusiness, 1999), p. xvi.

3. Ibid., p. xvii.

4. Michael Lewis, *Moneyball: The Art of Winning an Unfair Game* (New York: W. W. Norton, 2003), pp. 21–42.

5. Hans Bleichrodt, Jose Luis Pinto, and Peter P. Wakker, "Making Descriptive Use of Prospect Theory to Improve the Prescriptive Use of Expected Utility," *Management Science* 47, no. 11 (2001): 1499.

6. Daniel Kahneman and Amos Tversky, "Prospect Theory: An Analysis of Decision under Risk," *Econometrica* 47, no. 2 (1979): 274–80.

7. Brad M. Barber and Terrance Odean, "Individual Investors," in *Advances in Behavioral Finance*, vol. 2, ed. Richard H. Thaler (Princeton, NJ: Princeton University Press, 2005), pp. 550–53.

8. Board of Governors of the Federal Reserve System, *The Federal Reserve System: Purposes and Functions*, 9th ed. (2005), p. 15. http://www.federalreserve.gov/pf/pdf/pf_complete.pdf (accessed May 26, 2010).

9. Alberto Alesina et al., "Political Instability and Economic Growth," *Journal of Economic Growth* 1, no. 2 (1996): 1381.

10. Peter M. Lee, *Bayesian Statistics: An Introduction* (New York: Halsted Press, 1989), p. viii.

11. Claude Halstead van Tyne, *The Loyalists in the American Revolution* (Honolulu: University Press of the Pacific, 2004), pp. 5–6.

12. Ron Chernow, *Alexander Hamilton* (New York: Penguin Books, 2004), p. 49.

13. Thomas S. Kuhn, *The Structure of Scientific Revolutions* (Chicago: University of Chicago Press, 1970), pp. 150–52.

14. Alex Taylor III, "Toyota: The Birth of the Prius," *Fortune*, February 21, 2006. http://money.cnn.com/2006/02/17/news/companies/mostadmired_fortune_toyota/index.htm (accessed May 29, 2010).

15. Nathan Rosenberg, *Inside the Black Box: Technology and Economics* (New York: Cambridge University Press, 1982), p. 110.

16. Kenneth Arrow, "The Economic Implications of Learning by Doing," *Review of Economic Studies* 29, no. 3 (1962): 155–73.

17. "The Changing Structure of the Electric Power Industry: An Update" (Energy Information Administration, 2000), pp. 111–17. http://www.eia.doe.gov/cneaf/electricity/chg_stru_update/update2000.pdf.

18. Martin Curd and J. A. Cover, eds., *Philosophy of Science: The Central Issues* (New York: W. W. Norton, 1998), p. 79.

19. Boyan Jovanovic, "Moore's Law and Learning by Doing," *Review of Economic Dynamics* 5 (2002): 346.

20. Author's calculations. "Changing Structure of the Electric Power Industry" (see note 17), pp. 111–17.

21. http://www.indianapolismotorspeedway.com/var/assets/stats/500/indianapolis_500_race_winners.pdf (accessed May 27, 2010).

22. Rosenberg, *Inside the Black Box*, pp. 62–63.

23. http://www.ornl.gov/sci/techresources/Human_Genome/project/privatesector.shtml (accessed May 27, 2010).

24. John Archibald Wheeler, "Albert Einstein," in *The World Treasure of Physics, Astronomy, and Mathematics*, ed. Timothy Ferris (Boston: Back Bay Books, 1991), p. 572.

25. Henry Petroski, *Invention by Design: How Engineers Get from Thought to Thing* (Cambridge, MA: Harvard University Press, 1996), pp. 8–42.

26. Eric von Hippel and Marcie Tyre, "How 'Learning by Doing' is Done: Problem Identification in Novel Process Equipment," *Research Policy* (1995): 1–12.

27. Eric von Hippel, *Democratizing Innovation* (Cambridge, MA: MIT Press, 2005), p. 22.

CHAPTER 7: Emergent Properties of Revolutions

1. http://www.intercult.su.se/cultaptation/tournament_details.php (accessed May 28, 2010).

2. http://www.intercult.su.se/cultaptation/tournament/Social_Learning_Strategies_Tournament_Final_Results_release.pdf (accessed May 28, 2010).

3. Sushi Bikhchandani, David Hirshleifer, and Ivo Welch, "A Theory of Fads, Fashion, Custom, and Cultural Change as Informational Cascades," *Journal of Political Economy* 100, no. 5 (1992): 994.

4. Martin Curd and J. A. Cover, eds., *Philosophy of Science: The Central Issues* (New York: W. W. Norton, 1998), p. 79.

5. Thomas A. Burnham, Judy K. Frels, and Vijay Mahajan, "Consumer Switching Costs: A Typology, Antecedents, and Consequences," *Journal of the Academy of Marketing Science* 31, no. 2 (2003): 112.

6. Craig R. Fox and Amos Tversky, "Ambiguity Aversion and Comparative Ignorance," in Daniel Kahneman and Amos Tversky, eds., *Choices, Values, and Frames* (Cambridge: Cambridge University Press, 2000), p. 529.

7. Paul Slovic, "The Construction of Preference" in Kahneman and Tversky, *Choices, Values, and Frames* (see note 6), p. 498.

8. Stephen Jay Gould, *The Structure of Evolutionary Theory* (Cambridge, MA: Belknap Press of Harvard University Press, 2002), p. 13.

9. Niles Eldredge and Stephen J. Gould, "Punctuated Equilibria: An Alternative to Phyletic Gradualism," in *Models in Paleobiology*, ed. Thomas J. M. Schopf (San Francisco: Freeman, Cooper, 1972), p. 87.

10. Ibid., p. 84.

11. Niles Eldredge et al., "The Dynamics of Evolutionary Stasis," *Paleobiology* 31, no. 2 (2005): 136.

12. Ricardo J. Caballero and Mohamad L. Hammour, "Institutions, Restructuring, and Macroeconomic Performance," in *Advances in Macroeconomic Theory*, ed. Jacques Dreze (New York: Palgrave, 2001), pp. 171–93.

13. Ibid.

14. http://www.nber.org/cycles.html (accessed May 28, 2010).

15. Ibid.

16. Author calculations. http://money.cnn.com/magazines/fortune/fortune500/2010/snapshots/2255.html (accessed May 28, 2010).

17. Caballero and Hammour, "Institutions, Restructuring, and Macroeconomic Performance," pp. 171–93.

18. Arch Puddington, "Freedom in the World 2010: Erosion of

Freedom Intensifies," Freedom House. http://www.freedomhouse
.org/uploads/fiw10/FIW_2010_Overview_Essay.pdf (accessed May 28, 2010).

19. Raghuram Iyengar, Christophe van den Bulte, and Thomas W. Valente, "Opinion Leadership and Social Contagion in New Product Diffusion," *Marketing Science Institute Report* (2008): 4.

20. http://c0688662.cdn.cloudfiles.rackspacecloud.com/down loads-pdf-release-bloom-foundation-customer-2–24–10_1.pdf (accessed May 28, 2010).

21. Jacob Goldenberg et al., "The Role of Hubs in the Adoption Process," *Journal of Marketing* 73, no. 2 (2009): 8.

22. Lada A. Adamic et al., "Search in Power-Law Networks," *Physical Review E* 64, no. 4 (2001): 64.

23. Stanley Milgram, "The Small-World Problem," *Psychology Today* 1, no. 1 (1967): 64.

24. Ibid., p. 65.

25. Jeffrey Travers and Stanley Milgram, "An Experimental Study of the Small-World Problem," *Sociometry* 32, no. 4 (2009): 442.

26. Michael Porter, *On Competition* (Boston: Harvard Business Review Book, 1998), p. 207.

CHAPTER 8: Predicting Innovation Adoption

1. Vijay Mahajan, Eitan Muller, and Frank M. Bass, "New Product Diffusion Models in Marketing: A Review and Directions for Research," *Journal of Marketing* 54 (1990): 2.

2. Vijay Mahajan, Eitan Muller, and Yoram Wind, "New Product Diffusion Models: From Theory to Practice," in *New Product Diffusion Models* (New York: Springer, 2000), p. 3.

3. Vijay Mahajan and Robert A. Peterson, *Models for Innovation Diffusion* (Newbury Park, CA: Sage Publications, 1985), p. 30.

4. Mahajan, Muller, and Bass, "New Product Diffusion Models in Marketing," p. 2.

5. Rodrigo Costas, Thed N. van Leeuwen, and Anthony F. J. van Raan, "Is Scientific Literature Subject to a 'Sell-by-Date'? A General

Methodology to Analyze the 'Durability' of Scientific Documents," *Journal of the American Society for Information Science and Technology* 61, no. 2 (2009): 329–39.

6. http://www.ssrn.com/ (accessed May 29, 2010).

7. http://hq.ssrn.com/rankings/Ranking_display.cfm?Request Timeout=5000&TRN_ gID=10&TMY_gID=1&order=ASC&runid =6373 (accessed May 29, 2010).

8. http://scm.ncsu.edu/public/facts/facs030820.html (accessed May 29, 2010).

9. Vicki G. Morwitz and David Schmittlein, "Using Segments to Improve Sales Forecasts Based on Purchase Intent: Which 'Intenders' Actually Buy?" *Journal of Marketing Research* 29 (1992): 391.

10. http://www.imdb.com/title/tt0329910/ (accessed May 29, 2010).

11. Frederick F. Reichheld, "The One Number You Need to Grow," *Harvard Business Review* (December 2003): 50.

12. Ibid., p. 51.

13. Drazen Prelec, "A Bayesian Truth Serum for Subjective Data," *Science* 306 (2004): 462.

14. Ibid., p. 465.

15. Drazen Prelec and Ray Weaver, "Truthful Answers Are Surprisingly Common: Experimental Tests of the Bayesian Truth Serum," p. 7. http://www.rayweaver.net/hbsfiles/truthtelling_incentives.pdf (accessed May 29, 2010).

16. Drazen Prelec and H. Sebastian Seung, "An Algorithm That Finds Truth Even If Most People Are Wrong," p. 7. http://www.sabanciuniv .edu/HaberlerDuyurular/Documents/DD20100317104512/PrelecSeu ngDistributionShort.pdf (accessed May 29, 2010).

17. Ibid.

18. Steven D. Levitt, "Why Are Gambling Markets Organized So Differently from Financial Markets?" *Economic Journal* 114 (2004): 231.

19. http://abetterguess.com (accessed May 29, 2010).

CHAPTER 9: The Universal Constant

1. Philippe Aghion and Peter Howitt, "A Model of Growth through Creative Destruction," *Econometrica* 60, no. 2 (1992): 323–24.

2. Clayton M. Christensen and Michael E. Raynor, *The Innovator's Solution: Creating and Sustaining Successful Growth* (Boston: Harvard Business School Press, 2003), p. 34.

3. Laurence Prusak and Thomas H. Davenport, "Who Are the Gurus' Gurus?" *Harvard Business Review* (December 2003): 14–15.

4. Peter F. Drucker, *Managing for Results* (New York: Harper & Row, 1986), cover quote.

5. Ibid., p. 174.

6. http://www.homeofheroes.com/presidents/speeches/kennedy _space.html (accessed May 30, 2010).

7. Alexander Kotov, "Strategy and Tactics of Attack on the King," in *The Art of the Middle Game*, trans. H. Golombeck (New York: Dover Publications, 1964), p. 30.

8. Pat Langley et al., *Scientific Discovery: Computation Explorations of the Creative Process* (Cambridge, MA: MIT Press, 1992), p. 305.

9. http://www.pocketgadget.org/2008/01/14/serendipity-10 -accidental-inventions/ (accessed May 30, 2010).

INDEX